RUDE
FOOD

RUDE FOOD

First published in 2003
This revised edition copyright © Summersdale Publishers Ltd, 2016

Vector illustrations © Shutterstock

With research by Luke Cox and Abi McMahon

Summersdale Publishers Ltd
46 West Street
Chichester
West Sussex
PO19 1RP
UK

www.summersdale.com

Printed and bound in the Czech Republic

ISBN: 978-1-84953-931-9

Substantial discounts on bulk quantities of Summersdale books are available to corporations, professional associations and other organisations. For details contact Nicky Douglas by telephone: +44 (0) 1243 756902, fax: +44 (0) 1243 786300 or email: nicky@summersdale.com.

RISQUÉ RECIPES FOR SAUCY SUPPERS

RUDE FOOD

SAM COX

summersdale

CONTENTS

ABOUT THIS BOOK

If you want to cook to impress a loved one; or to turn a friend into a lover; or a stranger into a friend, then these recipes will only be as helpful as this advice: all you have to remember is that food, like life, should be about pleasure. If you keep that in mind while you cook, eat, chat and wash up (perhaps the next morning?), then I guarantee nothing can go wrong: you may burn the cheese sauce a little, or neglectfully overcook your scallops – but, really, who cares?

The aim of this book is to help you keep the pleasure and fun of cooking and eating on the metaphorical front burner. I've provided some ideas for romantic and clandestine meals that range from the teasingly erotic to the downright rude, and a dictionary of filthy food from which you can devise your own naughty nibbles and saucy snacks.

Most of the recipes in this book are for two, naturally, but sometimes, when more of an orgy is in order, the measures are for more. Feel free to change the quantities of ingredients to cater for whomever you happen to be entertaining…

Remember: it's not the food that makes the meal, it's the person you're with. So please make sure you eat while you have fun – and have fun while you eat.

WHAT IS RUDE FOOD?

Food can be as rude as you want it to be, and in your teasing, tasting, licking and slurping experiments you've probably already discovered that the humblest of dishes can be the most unexpectedly erotic, while a crudely wrinkled turnip, genetically modified to resemble a giant phallus, may do nothing for you at all.

The fact is that what turns us on is as diverse as what makes us laugh, cry or want to kick someone, so whatever anyone tells you about the aphrodisiac properties of food, remember that experimentation is the key – and don't believe for a minute that just because you find eating cold baked beans an intensely spiritual and earth-shattering experience you are some sort of food pervert. Well, you are, but don't let it bother you. After all, it is only through eating a selection of bizarre and unlikely delicacies through the ages that we have arrived at our present understanding of what rude food actually is.

Throughout human history, we have endeavoured to discover ways to improve our sexual prowess, to defrost the frigid and loosen our rigid inhibitions. As our lives, and especially our energetic sex lives, are dependent on food for survival, it isn't entirely surprising that these attempts have focused on what and how we eat.

The earliest principles of rude food worked on a simple premise: we are what we eat, so eating things that have huge, insatiable libidos will make us more like them – and if we eat things that are in some way deeply involved in the process of sex we'll be more like those things too. This led a bored Roman aristocracy to ingest huge quantities of genitalia in whatever form they could find them: monkeys' testicles, boars' penises, and even deer vulva – no animal was safe from the rude food quest of these supposedly civilised people.

From this dark and unenlightened age of rude food experimentation, a new philosophy evolved. Bored with centuries of chowing down boar cock with no discernible results, the Western world – in a flash of inspiration – decided this: it doesn't have to be the sex bit that you eat, it just has to look like it. Suddenly the hitherto undiscovered properties of a range of unlikely and otherwise unexciting foods were unleashed upon an unsuspecting public: oysters became the new black; melted butter was longingly teased from the drooping ends of asparagus spears; turnips and onions were looked at and handled in new ways they'd never before experienced, and which they rather enjoyed. These principles are still, in one way or another, with us today. We don't seriously believe that if something looks like a willy it will give us the raging horn, but if it works, roll with it. Hence you'll find this recipe book chock-full of suggestions involving artichokes (peel back the outer leaves to reveal the fruit within), saucily voluptuous avocados, prodigiously nipple-like strawberries, gently curving bananas, and so on and so forth.

All this, though, overlooks the most important principle of all rude food experimentation through the ages. It was largely an ignorance of the tenets of Eastern philosophy that condemned the Ancient Roman civilisation to all those centuries of eating wholly unsavoury concoctions: while Romans were busy hacking off the private parts of whatever they'd caught that morning, the Buddhist, Hindu and Islamic quarters of the world were revelling in the discoveries they'd made about the internal effects food has on the brain and the body – and were having some pretty good sex while they were at it. They learnt all about pine nuts, and gingko, and coffee, and garlic, and ginger, and fennel, and honey, and chillies, and figs – and decided that while none of these things looked anything like their own body parts should look (well, perhaps the figs did, on a bad day), they were definitely doing something.

Today the question of whether there are any true natural aphrodisiacs is as clouded in folklore and myth as it was then, with scientists, the grumpy lot that they are, deciding they have better things to do than mess about with lobsters and truffles and placebos. We do know, however, that a healthy body equals a healthy mind, that a combination of both has a positive influence on our romantic and sexual ventures, and also that some foods contain vitamins and minerals that can help us with that extra touch of perkiness and zing just when we need it.

So, my disciple, I suspect you are no closer to knowing what rude food is than you were when you started reading. My advice is: journey through a world of saucy starters, irrepressibly frisky fish, incredibly naughty mains and frankly cheeky desserts, and only then shall you find those first steps on the path to enlightenment towards the nirvana of the answer you desire. Or, failing that, cook up a few of the recipes, browse through the A–Z of rudeness at the back, and have a bit of fun in the kitchen while you do it. The world of rude food is now, officially, your oyster.

THE SCIENCE BIT

If anyone tells you that cooking is a precise science they're either lying or spend all their time in the kitchen with their eyes glued to the pages of a cookery book, rarely looking up to fish out that tasty morsel lurking at the back of the fridge that would go oh-so-well with whatever it is they're knocking up out of Delia. I don't think there's a single recipe in the whole world that could be completely scuppered by an overly hearty application of your favourite herb, the grossly negligent omission of a cheese you consider ghastly, or the shock and unscripted inclusion of something random from the depths of your condiment drawer (the exception seeming to be cake-baking which, even if you follow the recipe precisely, seems to be a skill people only acquire with age). That said, one shouldn't ignore a recipe entirely, but instead use it as a handy guide, or a list of suggestions – in the spaces between the lines experiment away and, if you make an earth-shatteringly tasty discovery, pretend it's what you intended all along. It's a principle that works for me, anyway.

So assume the measurements in this book to be approximate and don't stress yourself out if you are a little over the recommended amount of monkfish and two ounces under on the potatoes – I have faith it will all come right in the end. Similarly, with the cooking times, different pieces of kit will cook at different speeds and you may, with experience, want to tinker about with the timing to make life easier for yourself. The preparation times quoted are based on my own chopping, peeling and coring speeds, which I hope you will find to be reassuringly unprofessional and pedestrian.

Oven temperatures are given in Celsius and Fahrenheit, but for those with plain old gas marks, here's a conversion table (all temperatures are approximate):

Fahrenheit	Celsius	Gas Mark
300	150	2
325	160–70	3
350	180	4
375	190	5
400	200	6
425	220	7
450	230	8

The technology you'll need to employ to be a rude food chef also shouldn't give you too much of a passion-killing headache. You'll find no recipes that require you to possess a 6-inch ramekin (does anyone have a ramekin?!), and I'd like to think you'd find a way to cook most of these recipes if all you had access to was your granddad's wartime penknife and a fire. On occasion you'll need a food processor, even if it's one of those handheld zizzer things (which are incredibly useful). Oh, and a syringe, which playfully pops up in the Decadent Desserts chapter. I'd also advise investing in a good, robust pepper mill (go for an extra-large one if you're an insatiable pepper-lover – pleasingly firm in the hand) and salt cellar, as it's so much nicer to grind the stuff fresh. I've tried to avoid chef jargon at all times, but I will ask you to zest occasionally. This just means rubbing the skin of the citrus fruit over a cheese grater to get tiny slivers of the tangy peel.

Do remember that presentation means a lot to people. We eat and taste with our eyes, as much as we do with our mouths and noses. To get the most from your food, invest in some attractive crockery, cutlery to match and, of course, some candles, because everything in the world (and especially my cooking) looks better by candlelight.

The icons used in this book will help you see at a glance the basic info for each recipe:

 How many people this dish serves

 How long the dish takes to prepare (in minutes)

 How long the dish takes to cook (in minutes)

SAFE AND HEALTHY EATING AND PLAYING

There are worse betrayals you could offer a lover than food poisoning. However, nothing kills passion faster than stomach cramps, diarrhoea and a call to your GP, so for the sake of both your relationship and your health, stick to these simple DOs and DON'Ts when preparing, cooking, eating and playing with food.

DO wash your hands before preparing or cooking food.

DON'T allow raw meat, fish and seafood to come into contact with cooked food, vegetables, salads, etc. Use separate chopping boards and utensils for preparing raw meat, or wash them well between uses. DO wash your hands well if they've come into contact with raw meat BEFORE you handle any other implements or food.

DO thoroughly cook meat before it is served. For chicken, pork and reformed meats (i.e. sausages and burgers) this means the meat must be cooked through. Test chicken and pork with a skewer or knife to check no pink colour remains and, in the case of chicken, check that the juices run clear. With sausages and burgers, I advise cooking an extra one which you can slice in half to check it is thoroughly cooked: a small financial penalty to pay for peace of mind. Steaks and other cuts of red meat should be cooked so that no pink colour remains on the outside.

DO wash vegetables before cooking and salad vegetables before serving – I'd do this even if you're buying packet vegetables that say they're pre-washed. A salad-spinner is therefore a great piece of kit well worth investing in. Similarly, DO thoroughly rinse fruit before you eat it or cook it.

DO buy the freshest food available, be it meat, fish, vegetables or dairy products. Freshness will always taste better, and in the case of fish, which in some instances can be served raw, is your guarantee of safety. DO try to buy free-range eggs – not only are you doing your bit for animal welfare, but they taste better too.

DON'T let your food get too close to you or your partner's genitals, and certainly never let it 'inside'. Playing with your food is healthy – and fun – but remember to treat your body with respect. Food, especially spreadable food, can be hard to remove and cause irritation or even infection. This is an especial risk for ladies, but the uncircumcised gentleman also needs to be careful with food coming into contact with his foreskin. It goes without saying that you should be particularly careful with spicy foods, but it probably bears making it explicit anyway. No one wants fun time to be abbreviated by a swift and alarmed dash to the bathroom to splash their bits with cold water. On that note, also be careful with heat. If it's too hot for your mouth, it's certainly too hot for your more delicate areas.

Rabelais famously wrote: 'The appetite grows by eating.' DO eat a healthy, balanced diet to ensure a healthy sexual appetite. Not just your sexual performance but your general well-being, weight, mental alertness and energy levels will be affected in the long term by the food you consume. DO eat a good balance of proteins, fats and carbohydrates, and avoid eating highly sugary foods too often. Also make sure you get plenty of fresh fruit and vegetables. DON'T be a crazy health freak – fat is not, in itself, bad for you: you need some as part of a balanced diet and avoiding it completely will be detrimental to your health.

For a more comprehensive guide to safe eating – especially if you find yourself storing and cooking large amounts of food – DO invest in a copy of the latest edition of *Essential Food Hygiene*, published by the Royal Society for Public Health.

Now, that's the sensible bit out of the way: go out there and get cooking…

SAUCY STARTERS AND SEXY SOUPS

A speedy encounter with your kitchen worktop has its pleasures: your hunger is quickly sated, you don't have to wipe down the dining-room table afterwards and you only have to wash up a few sets of plates. But can true satisfaction come without anticipation? You don't know how hungry you truly are until you've whetted your appetite. Here are a few suggestions for teasing plates that are just enough to leave you wanting more.

SIMPLE, SEXY AVOCADO VINAIGRETTE

2 | 10 | 0

Avocado flesh should be creamy and nutty. To ensure your fruit is ripe, cup it in the palm of your hand, fingers spread wide around its width (you wouldn't want to cause bruising), and squeeze it firmly but gently. There should be a little give, just enough to let you know it's good to go.

INGREDIENTS

½ tsp Worcestershire sauce
½ tsp English mustard powder
½ tsp sugar
½ tsp salt
2 drops Tabasco sauce
4 tbsp extra virgin olive oil
2 tbsp white wine vinegar
2 ripe avocados
¼ iceberg lettuce, to garnish

METHOD

→ Mix together the mustard powder, Worcestershire sauce, Tabasco, salt and sugar in a bowl. Gradually drizzle in the olive oil, beating the mixture with a fork as you add it to keep it smooth. When all the oil's been added, do the same with the vinegar, adding it slowly until the vinaigrette begins to thicken a little.

→ Halve and stone the avocados. To do this, slip the avocado lengthways onto a sharp blade and rotate the avocado 360° with the blade always in contact with the stone. Rotate the halves in opposite directions and the fruit will fall in two. If your avocado is ripe enough, the stone will pop out under gentle pressure from a tsp.

→ Place the halves in bowls, stone side up, and fill the wells to brimming point with the vinaigrette dressing. Scatter a little finely chopped lettuce over the avocados and serve immediately.

PARSNIP FRITTERS WITH SWEET CITRUS SAUCE

If it's cold outside, you'll be begging for a large root to warm you up on the inside. The sticky citrus sauce will add some zest to this familiar, but not vanilla, dish.

INGREDIENTS

For the fritters:
4 medium parsnips,
    or 2 particularly big ones
1 large egg
2 tbsp single cream
2 tbsp white wine
Pinch of freshly
    ground nutmeg
2 oz / 50 g butter or
    2 tbsp cooking oil
Salt and black pepper,
    to season

For the sauce:
4 tsp caster sugar
2 oranges (1 to juice and
    zest, 1 to garnish)

METHOD

→ Wash and peel the parsnips and boil them in lightly salted water for 35–40 minutes. Drain well, then mash the parsnips together with the cream, wine, egg, seasoning and a tiny sprinkle of nutmeg (¼ tsp should do) until smooth and even. With lightly floured hands, shape the mash into six even-sized balls, and press each one down on a flat surface so the balls form thick, round patties.

→ Heat the butter or oil in a saucepan until just spitting, and fry the patties for 5 minutes each side or until a rich, golden brown. Drain them on kitchen towel. Meanwhile, heat the orange juice, zest and sugar in a small saucepan, stirring until the juice is simmering and the sugar has dissolved.

→ Arrange the fritters on a plate, interspersed with thin orange segments, drizzle the sauce over the top and serve whilst still hot.

CROSTINI ALLA CHIANTIGIANA (CHICKEN LIVER PÂTÉ ON TOAST)

Wine, liver, onion: the earthy flavours of this starter are straight out of the heart of rural Tuscany. Think cool linen, the warm summer breeze kissing hot skin and empty wine glasses abandoned on the balcony table.

INGREDIENTS

8 oz / 225 g chicken livers, washed and chopped
1 celery stalk, finely chopped
1 small carrot, peeled and finely chopped
1 small white onion, peeled and finely chopped
1 garlic clove, peeled and crushed

4 tbsp olive oil
2 oz / 50 g unsalted butter
4 tbsp dry white wine
Salt and black pepper, to season
1 loaf good white bread (e.g. French stick or ciabatta)

METHOD

→ Heat the oil and butter together in a heavy-based saucepan. When the butter has melted, add the chopped vegetables and the crushed garlic, and sauté them over a medium heat for 10 minutes, stirring frequently. Add the liver pieces and continue cooking and stirring for 4–5 minutes, or until the liver has cooked through (no pink colour will remain).

→ Pour the wine into the pan and turn the heat up a little, simmering the wine down until it has almost all evaporated. Remove the saucepan from the heat, cover and allow the contents to cool.

→ When cool, transfer the chicken mixture to a food processor, season generously and purée until smooth. Put the pâté in a suitable container and refrigerate for a good couple of hours before serving. It can be served up straight away but the flavour seems to develop with time, and preparing ahead allows you less stress later on.

→ When ready to serve, heat the oven to 200°C / 400°F, line a baking sheet with foil and place chunkily sliced rounds of bread on it. Brush them with a little oil and bake them for 10 minutes or so until golden (or, if feeling lazy and distinctly uncontinental, bung the bread in a toaster). Spread the toast with generous lashings of pâté and serve to your ravenous, oomph-lacking guests.

PRAWN AND
SESAME YIN YANG

2 | 10 | 15

Yin Yang: the head of the dark sinking onto the base of the light, the head of the light sinking onto the base of the dark. So do the flavours of mushroom and sesame mingle with the freshness of the prawns, parsley and lemon with this Cantonese starter.

INGREDIENTS

1 tbsp sesame oil
1 tbsp vegetable oil
6 oz / 150 g baby / button
    mushrooms
3 tbsp sesame seeds
1 lb / 500 g fresh, peeled
    prawns (or frozen, cooked
    if you must)

3 tbsp fresh parsley, chopped
2 tbsp Chinese wine (or sherry)
2 tbsp lemon juice
1 spring onion, finely
    chopped, to garnish

METHOD

→ Heat the oils together in a saucepan (or a wok, if you want to look the part) over a medium–high heat. Cook the mushrooms briskly until slightly browned, and then add the sesame seeds and prawns.

→ Fry for 8–10 minutes, stirring well, then add the wine, lemon juice and parsley. Stir well, remove from the heat and serve hot in two small bowls, topping each with a smattering of chopped spring onion.

PRAWN AND SAFFRON DIPPING AND SCOOPING PASTE

The long, red stigma of the saffron crocus thrusts from the centre of its purple blossom and, when ground up, is the most expensive spice in the world. It has a complex flavour and a bitter undertone that lingers on the tongue after you've swallowed.

INGREDIENTS

8 oz / 225 g cooked and
    peeled prawns
2 large egg yolks
½ pint / 300 ml single or
    reduced fat cream
½ pint / 300 ml dry white wine

1 fish stock cube
A good pinch of saffron
    strands
2 tbsp fresh coriander,
    chopped

METHOD

→ Whizz together half the prawns, and the egg yolks, saffron, cream and wine with the fish stock cube in a food processor until smooth and even. Transfer the mixture to a heavy-based saucepan and heat gently, stirring constantly, until the mixture begins to thicken – taking care not to boil it.

→ Add the rest of the prawns to the pan, mix well to heat through, and serve with a handful of fresh, chopped coriander. Another great dish to get truly messy with – fingers a necessity, breadsticks optional.

TANTALISING TROUT MOUSSE

The light, fishy flavour of this mousse dances delicately on your tongue, whetting your appetite before you tuck into meatier dishes.

INGREDIENTS

1 lb / 500 g fresh trout, gutted
4 oz / 100 g potatoes (fluffy
   ones like King Edward or
   Desiree)
1–2 oz / 25–50 g unsalted
   butter
Juice of 2 lemons
4 tbsp cognac
2 ripe avocados (1 for garnish)
1 tsp cayenne pepper
Salt and black pepper,
   to season

METHOD

→ Cook the trout by grilling it for 2–3 minutes on each side under a medium–high heat or, if feeling lazy, by microwaving it in a non-metallic dish for 4 minutes on high. Remove the head, tail and bones (this is marginally easier to do when cooked).

→ Peel and boil the potatoes in lightly salted water until soft and mashable. Melt half the butter in a pan, and meanwhile whizz together the trout flesh, one avocado, lemon juice, cognac and potatoes in a food processor until smooth and fluffy. Add the remaining butter, cayenne pepper and season generously with salt and pepper. Whizz in the processor again for 10–20 seconds.

→ Transfer the mousse to a bowl and let it cool in a refrigerator. Serve garnished with sliced avocado – a perfect dip for eating from hunks of crusty bread, fingers and lips.

CAVIAR KISSES

You'll first note the light, salty flavour of caviar as you take it into your mouth, then, as the eggs pop, a rich and slightly sweet flavour will ooze over your tongue, overpowering your senses.

INGREDIENTS

¼ pint / 150 ml sour cream
1 tbsp fresh chives, chopped
1 tbsp fresh dill, chopped (or
   1 tsp dried dill)
Black pepper, to season
1 cucumber
2 oz / 50 g caviar (such as red
   salmon caviar)
Fresh dill sprigs, to garnish
   (optional)

METHOD

→ In a bowl combine the sour cream, chives, dill and a twist of black pepper, and mix well. Wash and trim the cucumber and slice it into rounds about ¼ inch / ½ cm thick.

→ To assemble the kisses, simply spread each cucumber round with the sour cream and herb mixture, topping each slice with a small spoonful of caviar and a sprig of fresh dill.

→ For an extra touch (to show you care), serve with hot buttered toast trimmed into heart shapes.

ROUGH-CUT GUACAMOLE

There is no cooking time with this classic Mexican starter, so it's the perfect dish to make when your lover arrives. Share the preparation duty and enjoy your fingers slipping over each other as you blend the ingredients, wet with the juice of the lime and lightly tingling with the sting of chilli.

INGREDIENTS

3 ripe avocados
1 small green chilli, deseeded
   and finely chopped
1 large garlic clove, crushed
1 dash Tabasco sauce
Juice of 1 lime
½ red onion, peeled and
   roughly chopped
2 tbsp fresh coriander, washed
   and roughly chopped
½ tsp paprika

METHOD

→ Halve the avocados, remove the stones and scoop the flesh out into a bowl. Mash the flesh with a fork and mix in the chilli, lime juice, garlic and Tabasco. Continue to mash until the mixture is smooth, then mix in the red onion. Stir well, cover and refrigerate for 1 hour.

→ Just before serving, stir in the coriander, garnish with a sprinkling of paprika and serve with tortilla chips or vegetable batons to dip – or just lick it seductively from your lover's fingers.

CHILLI AND BASIL
TOMATO SALSA

The chilli of this salsa nips at your mouth and stops the flavours of this dish from being too safe and predictable.

INGREDIENTS

1 lb / 500g fresh, ripe plum tomatoes
1 small white onion, peeled and roughly chopped
2 large garlic cloves, peeled
2 tbsp fresh basil (one big handful)
2 tbsp extra virgin olive oil

1 drop Tabasco or pepper sauce
Salt and black pepper, to season
1 green chilli, deseeded and finely chopped
1 red chilli, deseeded and finely chopped

METHOD

→ Firstly, dispense with the tomato skins: using a small, sharp knife remove the hard nodules where the tomatoes were attached to the stalk, then immerse the tomatoes in freshly boiled water. After a minute or so, remove the tomatoes with a slotted spoon and with a little pressure the skins should fall away. Whizz the garlic, onion and basil in a food processor in short bursts until finely minced. Halve the skinned tomatoes and add them to the mix: again, use short bursts so the salsa has a rough, coarse texture.

→ Turn the processor to its slowest setting and slowly drizzle in the olive oil until well blended, then add a tiny dash of Tabasco or pepper sauce and a healthy whack of salt and pepper. Finally, stir in the thinly sliced chillies.

→ The salsa can be served immediately, with the obligatory dipping delights of tortilla chips, but the flavour tends to develop a little if it is left covered and refrigerated for an hour or so beforehand.

SPINACH, APPLE AND CORIANDER SOUP

Start your evening with a spot of original sin with this apple-tinged soup. There's nothing quite as enticing as a pair of smooth, rosy apples, so let this starter tempt you into more.

INGREDIENTS

3 cooking apples (but any
    apples can be used)
2 oz / 50 g unsalted butter
12 oz / 300 g spinach, washed
    and chopped
Salt and black pepper,
    to season

¼ tsp nutmeg
Juice of 1 lemon
4 tbsp fresh coriander,
    chopped
¼ pint / 150 ml single or
    double cream (optional)

METHOD

→ Peel and core the apples, then chop them into small cubes. Melt the butter in a large saucepan over a low heat, add the apples and gently sauté them for 5 minutes, or until they start to brown and tenderise a little.

→ Add the spinach, ¾ pint / 400 ml water and season generously, also adding a small pinch of nutmeg. (If you want a really smooth soup, allow the mixture to cool and then liquidise it before returning it to the pan.) Turn up the heat and bring the liquid to boiling point, then turn it back down, cover the saucepan and simmer the ingredients for 20 minutes. Just before serving, stir in the lemon juice.

→ Spoon out the soup into two suitable bowls and top each with a good fistful of chopped coriander and, if liked, a drizzle of fresh cream.

FRENCH ONION SOUP

2 | 25 | 60

French soup, French kisses, French letters – the French are prepared for every element of a romantic evening. Bring the country of love into your kitchen, and later, maybe other rooms…

INGREDIENTS

2 oz / 50 g unsalted butter
1 lb / 500 g white onions,
    peeled and finely chopped
2 tbsp plain flour
1 pint / 600 ml beef stock
2 tsp salt
Black pepper, to season
¼ pint / 150 ml brandy
½ French stick
2 oz / 50 g Gruyère cheese,
    grated
2 oz / 50 g Parmesan cheese,
    grated
2 tbsp extra virgin olive oil

METHOD

→ In a large saucepan, and over a low heat, melt the butter. Add the onions and cook for 8–10 minutes, or until soft. Sift the flour into the saucepan, coating the onions, then add ¼ pt / 150 ml of the beef stock and continue to cook until the mixture thickens a little. When it has, add the salt, a twist or three of pepper, the brandy and the remainder of the stock.

→ Turn up the heat and bring the liquid to a boil, then turn the heat back down, cover the saucepan and let it simmer away for 30 minutes, stirring occasionally. While it gently bubbles, heat the oven to 200°C / 400°F, slice the French stick into thin rounds and bake the slices in the oven for 10 minutes until crisp and dry.

→ To serve in the traditional (and impressive) manner, ladle the soup into bowls and cover it with a generous sprinkling of Gruyère cheese. Cover the Gruyère with two or three baked bread slices, gently drizzle olive oil over the bread, and top the bowl with the grated Parmesan. Place each bowl under a hot grill for 1 minute, and then serve immediately.

SPEEDY ASPARAGUS VELOUTÉ

A soup so soft and velvety you'll want to dip your fingers in instead of a spoon.

INGREDIENTS

1 lb / 500 g asparagus tips
¼ pint / 150 ml single cream
¼ pint / 150 ml chicken stock
1 egg yolk
Black pepper, to season
1 tbsp chives, chopped

METHOD

→ Trim and roughly chop the asparagus tips. Place them in a food processor and whizz until finely chopped. Add the cream, stock, egg yolk and a twist or three of ground pepper, replace the lid and continue to blend until smooth and even.

→ Transfer the liquid to a saucepan and heat gently for 10 minutes, taking care not to bring the soup to the boil. Serve immediately, garnished with a sprinkle of black pepper and a handful of chopped chives on the top of each bowl.

FENNEL, LIQUORICE AND PRAWN SOUP

The brown flower of the star anise hides its seed in its folds and it's from these that we get the toothsome flavour that mingles with the bulb of the fennel for this hot starter.

INGREDIENTS

1 lb / 500 g fennel bulb
½ pint / 300 ml dry white wine
1 chicken stock cube
4 oz / 100 g cooked prawns
¼ pint / 150 ml crème fraîche
2 tbsp Pernod, ouzo or other
   liquorice aperitif
Salt and black pepper, to
   season
Handful of chopped coriander,
   to garnish

METHOD

→ Trim the fennel stalks down to the bulb, removing and discarding any wilted outer layer, and chop the bulb into small cubes. If you bought a bulb with fennel leaves – a rarity in supermarkets – reserve the leaves to use as a garnish later. In a heavy-based pan, heat the white wine, ½ pint / 300 ml water and chicken stock together with the pieces of fennel until boiling. Boil for 5–7 minutes until it reduces a little, then transfer the mixture to a food processor and whizz it together until it forms a smooth purée.

→ Allow the mixture to cool, then return to the pan. Heat until simmering, but not boiling, then add the crème fraîche, Pernod and prawns, and mix together well, seasoning generously.

→ Serve hot with buttered toast and a sprinkling of the reserved fennel leaves to garnish – a smattering of fresh chopped coriander will serve just as well and will add a new, subtle flavour.

SWEET POTATO AND BASIL SOUP

4 | 25 | 30

The process of turning the flesh of these root vegetables tender and smothering them in milk and cream will get you and your kitchen hot and steamy.

INGREDIENTS

1 oz / 25 g unsalted butter
2 large onions, peeled and chopped
2 medium carrots, peeled and diced
1 large celery stalk, diced
4 large sweet potatoes
2 bay leaves
½ tsp dried thyme
Tiny pinch of nutmeg

1 vegetable stock cube
¾ pint / 200 ml semi-skimmed milk
Salt and black pepper, to season
6 tbsp fresh basil (2 big handfuls of leaves)
2 tbsp single cream
Basil sprigs, to garnish

METHOD

→ Melt the butter in a large, heavy-based saucepan over a low heat. Add the chopped onions, carrots and celery and gently sauté them until the onions begin to turn golden brown. Peel and chop the sweet potatoes into cubes and add them to the saucepan along with the bay leaves, thyme and nutmeg, the crumbled stock cube and enough cold water to just cover the vegetables. Turn up the heat and bring the water to the boil. Cover the pan and allow the contents to simmer for 15–20 minutes or until both the carrots and sweet potatoes are tender and fall apart easily when tested with a fork.

→ Drain the solid ingredients in a colander – with a bowl underneath to catch the stock – and place them in a food processor with 4 tbsp of the liquid. Whizz them together until you have a smooth and even purée. Return both the stock and purée to the original saucepan and stir them together well. Return to a low heat, gradually add the milk and season well. Simmer like this for 10 minutes, or until ready to serve. Wash, dry and chop the basil, then stir it into the soup 5 minutes before you serve up.

→ Serve in bowls with the crustiest, tastiest bread and, for an extra touch, a small swirl of single cream and a sprig of basil delicately balanced on top of the soup.

CROSTINI AI CARCIOFI (ARTICHOKE HEARTS ON TOAST)

Hearts don't have to be involved when it's a night in for two, but they are with this tangy Italian starter. But then, between artichoke hearts heated in their own juices and garlic rubbed into ciabatta by hand, who could resist?

INGREDIENTS

1 tin or jar artichoke hearts
3 oz / 75 g Parmesan cheese
1 loaf ciabatta bread / good
  white bread
1 large garlic clove
1 tbsp mayonnaise
Salt and black pepper,
  to season

METHOD

→ Empty the artichoke hearts into a saucepan with a little of the juice and heat them gently until they begin to soften. Add the Parmesan cheese and stir it in well, mushing the hearts with a fork to form a semi-mash. Heat through for 2 minutes, then remove from the hob.

→ Meanwhile, heat the grill and slice the ciabatta loaf into rounds 2 or 3 cm thick. Peel the garlic clove, bash it with the back of a knife, then rub the crushed clove all over the faces of the ciabatta slices. Grill them until they are golden.

→ When the artichoke mix has cooled a little, add the mayonnaise, a little salt and a big twist of pepper. Smear the mixture on the ciabatta slices and serve.

FRISKY FISH

You never forget your first fish. Some dive in as soon as they can get their hands on it, feasting on the salty white meat, seeking ever stronger flavours of the sea. Some are tentative at first, taking their oral pleasure elsewhere before finally succumbing to temptation; drawn in by a subtle scent or the sight of glistening flesh pillowed on a bed of salt or citrus. Whether a novice or enthusiast, the following pages are guaranteed to contain a recipe to satisfy your craving.

BLISSFUL BAKED TROUT

Engulf the trout in oil and roasted almonds, massaging until your fingers slip easily over the skin on top and soft underneath. The extra attention to detail will really bring this dish to a peak – the rewards will be in the tasting.

INGREDIENTS

2 tbsp flaked almonds
1 tbsp olive oil
2 trout fillets
Salt and black pepper,
*   to season*

METHOD

→ Preheat the oven to 200°C / 400°F. Mix the almonds and olive oil in a bowl, and spread the mixture over a foil-lined baking tray. Place on the top shelf of the oven for 10 minutes, or until the almonds start to sizzle and turn brown.

→ Remove the tray and scrape the almond flakes and oil into a bowl. Lay the trout fillets, skin side down, on the baking tray and season lightly with salt and pepper. Smear the flesh with the roasted almonds and oil.

→ Return the tray to the oven for 10 minutes – until the trout is delicate pink – and serve immediately.

MARINATED RED SNAPPER WITH COGNAC TAPENADE

2 | 10 | 25

There's something about the sweet, nutty taste of the red snapper that makes you want to bury your face in it and not stop until you're licking... the plate clean. Mouth-watering on its own, the real treat is when the red snapper is squirting with juices. Massage lemon juice, olive oil and your favourite herbs into the flesh, making sure you rub around the folds, and enjoy the contrast of flavours between the snapper and your tangy topping.

INGREDIENTS

For the fillets:
4 red snapper fillets
Salt and black pepper, to season
2 tbsp fresh basil, finely
   chopped
Zest of 1 lime
4 tbsp extra virgin olive oil

For the tapenade:
2 oz / 50 g black olives, pitted
2 tbsp cognac or brandy
1 tbsp capers
1 large garlic clove
Zest of 1 orange
Juice of 1 lime
2 tbsp extra virgin olive oil
2 tbsp Parmesan cheese
Salt and black pepper, to season

METHOD

→ Prepare the snapper fillets by rinsing them, patting them dry and then placing them, flesh side up, in a shallow dish, seasoning well with salt and pepper. Wash the basil and finely chop it, then mix it with the lime zest and spread both evenly over the fish. Pour the lime juice and then the olive oil over the fillets, cover the dish and leave it to marinate in a fridge for at least an hour before cooking.

→ Make the tapenade by whizzing together the cognac, olives, rinsed capers, garlic, orange zest, olive oil and Parmesan cheese in a food processor until smooth, and season to taste with salt and pepper.

→ Heat a griddle pan (or a frying pan, with no oil needed) over a high heat, remove the snapper fillets from the marinade, and cook them for no more than 1½ minutes on each side, searing the outside of the fish. Remove the fish from the pan and lay them in a shallow baking dish. Top each fillet with a generous smear of tapenade, transfer the dish to the oven and bake for 20 minutes at 200°C / 400°F. Serve fresh from the oven with some light, tasty vegetables, such as broccoli or French beans.

GALICIAN THYME-BAKED HAKE (MERLUZA À LA GALLEGA)

The more pleasure the better, which is why four participants are better than two. Invite some intimate friends for an evening of fishy dishes. This one's a slow burner, not for the wham, bam, thank you ma'am school of chef. Just wait until the flavour explosion and there'll be hands everywhere, trying to get just a little bit more.

INGREDIENTS

1 lb / 500g hake fillets
2 lb / 1 kg floury potatoes, such as King Edward and Maris Piper
2 oz / 50 g unsalted butter
2 tbsp olive oil
6 oz / 150 g red onions, finely chopped
1 large garlic clove

1 tbsp fresh parsley, chopped
1 tsp paprika
1 tbsp flour
2 tbsp fresh thyme, chopped
2 bay leaves
1 tsp green peppercorns
Salt, to season
Thyme sprigs, to garnish

METHOD

→ Rinse the hake fillets well under cold water then pat them dry with kitchen towel. Cut the fillets into thick slices and leave the slices refrigerated in a covered dish. Peel and chop the potatoes into thin rounds.

→ Heat the oil and butter in a large, heavy-based saucepan over a low heat, and gently fry the onions, stirring continuously, until they begin to turn golden brown. Crush and add the garlic along with the parsley and paprika, then add the potato slices. Sift the flour into the saucepan and continue to heat, turning the temperature up a little and stirring continuously.

→ When the potato rounds begin to turn a little translucent and brown at the edges, add cold water to the saucepan until the water just covers the contents. Add a good pinch of salt, the peppercorns, bay leaves and chopped thyme. Bring the liquid to the boil then cover and allow it to simmer for 15 minutes.

→ After this stew has bubbled away for a quarter of an hour, the potatoes should be tender. Using a slotted spoon, transfer all the solid contents to a large baking dish, spreading them evenly along its base and adding 3 tbsp of any remaining liquid. Top the dish with the hake slices, pressing them gently into the potato mixture, sprinkle a pinch of salt and a further tbsp of thyme over the fish, then place the dish in the oven for 10–15 minutes at 200°C / 400°F. Serve, garnished with a sprig or two of thyme, directly from the dish.

ORANGE AND FENNEL SEED CRUSTED HALIBUT

This is a plate where two become one; the halibut is plunged into a silken bath of egg and cream and then covered in fennel seed, sweet orange and breadcrumbs to create the perfect merging of flavours.

INGREDIENTS

Zest of 2 oranges
2 tsp fennel seed, ground
3 tbsp fresh white
    breadcrumbs
Salt and black pepper, to
    season
2 eggs
2 tbsp single cream
2 halibut fillets, boned
2 tbsp olive oil

METHOD

→ You will need two mixing bowls – in one, mix the orange zest, fennel, breadcrumbs, a generous pinch of salt and a good twist of black pepper. In the other, whisk together the eggs and cream. Immerse the halibut fillets in the egg and cream mixture, and then coat one side of the fillet with the breadcrumb, zest and fennel seed mixture.

→ Heat the oil in a frying pan over a medium heat. When hot, lay the halibut in the oil, crust side down, and fry until the breadcrumb crust goes golden brown (after 2–3 minutes). Flip the fillets over and continue to fry for a further 2–3 minutes, or until the flesh is firm to the touch. Serve with summer greens and buttery new potatoes.

IRISH GARLIC BUTTER MONKFISH TAIL

Some tails just need a good stuffing and monkfish is one of them. Fill with butter and roast until the slit is running with juices and your plate is wet with delicious flavour.

INGREDIENTS

3 oz / 75 g unsalted butter, plus 1 oz / 25 g to grease dish
2 large garlic cloves
1 tbsp fresh thyme, chopped
1 tbsp fresh marjoram, chopped
1 lb / 500 g monkfish tail fillets

2 eggs
2 tbsp single cream
4 tbsp plain flour
Salt and black pepper, to season
2 tbsp fresh white breadcrumbs
Juice of 1 lemon

METHOD

→ Leave the butter out overnight so it softens to room temperature (or soften the butter with short bursts in the microwave and mash it with a fork). Crush the garlic into a bowl, add the butter, marjoram and thyme, and mix the whole lot together well. Chill in the refrigerator until hard again.

→ While the oven heats to 200°C / 400°F, lay the monkfish tail fillets on a baking dish. With a sharp knife make a slit in each into which you can pack the garlic and herb butter, folding the slit up so the butter won't fall out. Beat the eggs and cream together in a bowl. In another bowl sift the flour and mix with a good pinch of salt and a generous twist of pepper, and in a third bowl place the breadcrumbs. Dip each fillet in the flour, then the egg and cream mix, and then the breadcrumbs, pressing the breadcrumbs into the flesh. Melt a little butter and use some of it to moisten the inside of the baking dish, and then return the fillets to it. Drizzle the rest of the butter, then the lemon juice, over the top of the fillets.

→ Place the baking dish in the oven, cooking the fillets for 30 minutes. Serve immediately with crusty bread to mop up the bubbly, buttery dribbles.

DIJON, CAPER AND GREEN PEPPER SKATE WINGS IN BEURRE NOISETTE

Endulging in the usual is all well and good, but sometimes you need a bit of edge to your evening. Add a dash of excitement with this skate main, flavoured with a lively combination of mustard, capers and peppercorns.

INGREDIENTS

2 oz / 50 g unsalted butter
2 large skate wings, skin removed
2 tbsp Dijon mustard
Salt and black pepper, to season
2 tsp capers
2 tsp green peppercorns

METHOD

→ Melt the butter in a pan over a very gentle heat. Brush the skate wings with a thin, even coating of the butter, then with another thin, even coating of Dijon mustard, and a sprinkle of seasoning. Grill the skate wings on a moderate heat for 2–3 minutes each side. While they are cooking, turn the heat up underneath the rest of the butter slightly. It should begin to turn a golden brown with small particles of a darker brown colour – when it does, remove it from the heat so as not to burn it.

→ When the skate wings are cooked, arrange them on plates with a sprinkling of drained capers and green peppercorns. Carefully pour the butter over the wings using a wooden spoon to keep the darker brown pieces in the pan. Top marks go to the chef who serves this up with a simple spoonful of buttery mash (see Buttery Mash with Parsley and Nutmeg recipe).

SEDUCTIVE SEAFOOD AND SUCCULENT SHELLFISH

Shellfish are some of the world's most powerful aphrodisiacs, with the most renowned being oysters – the food of lovers everywhere. Perhaps it's the way their succulent bodies nestle between the unfurled lips of the shell, or perhaps it's how plump they are and how smoothly they slide down our throats. Although oysters may be the most well-known for increasing libido, variety is the spice of life and so the following recipes contain dishes to make every mouth water.

SHERRY KING PRAWN TAPAS

The pink of perfectly done prawns should be that of the first blush of excitement or of wine-stained lips. Serve on a plate so you can share; no selfish eaters allowed.

INGREDIENTS

12 raw king tiger prawns
2 tbsp olive oil
4 tbsp sherry
Couple of drops of Tabasco
  sauce
Salt and black pepper, to
  season

METHOD

→ Prepare the prawns by shelling them, then scoring the back of each with a small sharp knife and carefully removing the dark intestinal tract. Alternatively, you could ask the fishmonger to do this for you, or buy ready-prepared prawns, but there's something immeasurably pleasing about doing this bit yourself.

→ Heat the oil in a frying pan or wok over a medium heat, add the prawns and fry for 3 minutes, or until entirely pink. Add the sherry and remove the pan from the heat. Throw in a couple of drops of Tabasco sauce, season well and serve in a dish for two to share.

→ You could just as easily make this dish with pre-cooked (pink) prawns – not as fun or as fresh, but still tasty. Simply cook for 1–2 minutes to heat the prawns through, otherwise use exactly the same method as above.

BELGIAN BEER AND BACON MUSSELS

Sometimes what a refined dish really wants is a bit of rough. In this recipe, the delicate mussels mingle with the guilty pleasure of beer and bacon for a really wild ride.

INGREDIENTS

12 oz / 300 g mussels
1 tbsp olive oil or vegetable oil
1 small white onion, chopped
1 large garlic clove, finely chopped or crushed
4 rashers smoked bacon (streaky or back), rind removed

4 tbsp beer (pick a lager for a lighter taste)
2 tbsp fresh basil, chopped
2 tbsp fresh thyme, chopped, to garnish

METHOD

→ Wash the mussels thoroughly, discarding any that are already open. Heat the oil in a large pan over a medium–high heat, and fry the onion, garlic and bacon for 5 minutes, or until golden. Add the mussels, beer, thyme and basil, and cover the pan with a tightly fitting lid. After 5 minutes remove the lid and spoon the mussels out into serving bowls, discarding any that have failed to open.

→ Mussels look wonderful and seductive as they are, but a sprig of thyme as a garnish for each bowl wouldn't go amiss, and remember to provide an empty bowl for the shells. If you really are bacon-mad, keep an additional rasher on hand and serve fried, chopped into small pieces and sprinkled on the mussels.

EXOTIC FRUIT AND SPICED SCALLOP SALAD

4 | 25 | 2-3

Bold, adventurous and healthy, this salad is the whole package if you're seeking to bring experimentation into your oven-life.

INGREDIENTS

1 small, ripe pineapple
1 red onion
1 red pepper
1 yellow pepper
1 small red chilli
1 large, ripe mango
8 oz / 225 g scallops
1 tbsp vegetable oil
1 oz / 25 g unsalted butter
4 large kale or lettuce leaves,
   to serve
1 tbsp fresh parsley, chopped
Juice of 1 lemon

METHOD

→ First do the chopping and dicing. Peel the pineapple, getting rid of all the remnants of spines, and cut the soft flesh away from the hard core. Slice into 1-cm cubes. Peel the onion, and slice it into thin strips; core the peppers and cut them into 1-cm hunks; and scrape all the seeds from the chilli and cut it into the finest strips possible. Finally peel the mango and cut the fibrous flesh away from the stone.

→ If necessary, prepare the scallops: in supermarkets, or from a fishmonger's, they may be ready-prepared, but if bought with the shells on you will need to rinse them well, pat them dry and pull away the hard muscular tissue that faces the red coral.

→ To make the salad, heat the oil and butter in a wok or frying pan over a medium heat. Add the peppers, chilli and onion and fry for 1 minute. Turn the heat up a touch and add the scallops. Fry for a further minute, then stir in the pineapple and parsley, and remove from the heat. Line a large dish with the kale or lettuce leaves and spoon the salad on top.

→ For the dressing, whizz together the mango flesh and lemon juice in a food processor until smooth. Spoon this mixture sparingly over the salad, and serve whilst still warm.

MOUTH-WATERING
STIR-FRY GINGER CRAB

Ginger and sherry impregnate crab meat with invigorating flavour in this Eastern-influenced dish. The complex flavours of this dish blossom as it slowly simmers, releasing enticing aromas that hang in the air.

INGREDIENTS

1 leek
4 large spring onions
4-cm piece of ginger, peeled
2 large cloves garlic
1 small red chilli
Good slug olive oil
2 crabs, dressed
2 tbsp oyster sauce
2 tbsp sherry
1 tbsp dark soy sauce
1 tbsp fresh coriander, finely
   chopped

METHOD

→ Slice the leek into fine, 4-cm-long slivers and the spring onions into 2-cm-long slivers. Finely chop, mince or grate the ginger, peel and crush the garlic cloves, and remove the seeds from the chilli and slice it finely.

→ Heat the oil in a wok or heavy frying pan over a medium–high heat. Add the ginger, garlic, leek and spring onions and cook for 2 minutes, taking care not to brown or burn them. Add the crab meat (white and brown meat), the oyster sauce, soy sauce, the sherry and 1 tbsp of cold water. Reduce the heat a touch and simmer the mixture for 3–4 minutes until it has reduced to a slightly thickened consistency.

→ If you have bought fresh crab, keep the shells, warm them under the hot tap, dry them well and serve the stir-fry using the shells as dishes. If not, serve on a bed of delicate, thin noodles (such as vermicelli), cooked according to packet instructions. Either way, serve topped with a sprinkle of freshly chopped coriander.

SUMPTUOUSLY STUFFED MEDITERRANEAN SQUID

Tentacles aren't for everyone but there's no shame here if they're what you want filling you up. Stuff the squid and then stuff yourself, until you're moaning because you feel full to the brim.

INGREDIENTS

2 large prepared squid

For the stuffing:
1 large garlic clove
4 spring onions, chopped
½ tbsp capers, chopped
½ tbsp black olives, chopped
3 tomatoes
Slug of olive oil
2 tbsp fresh parsley

2 tbsp fresh white
   breadcrumbs
Salt and black pepper, to
   season
1 egg yolk

For the mint oil:
4 tbsp olive oil
2 tbsp fresh mint

METHOD

→ It's best to make the stuffing first, but before you do, heat the oven to 150°C / 300°F. Prepare all the ingredients so you have them to hand: peel and crush or finely chop the garlic clove; roughly chop the spring onions, capers and black olives; and skin the tomatoes (by immersing them in freshly boiled water for a minute or so), removing and discarding the seeds and roughly chopping the flesh.

→ Heat 1 tbsp of olive oil in a heavy-based saucepan over a medium heat and fry the spring onions, garlic and – if your squid came with them – squid tentacles, roughly chopped, for 2 minutes. Remove the pan from the heat and allow the mixture to cool.

→ Mix together the parsley, breadcrumbs and tomatoes, a generous whack of salt and pepper and, when cool, the onion mixture. Add the egg yolk and beat it all together well so it binds. Lay the squid on a baking tray and gently score the flesh diagonally with a sharp knife: this helps to keep the flesh from splitting but is mainly aesthetic, so there's no need to do it if the flesh seems particularly thin.

→ Spoon the stuffing mixture into the squid body cavities, taking care not to overfill them: the flesh will expand slightly when cooking, so allow a little bit of room. Pin the ends of the squid with cocktail sticks so none of the stuffing can escape. Place the squid in the centre of the preheated oven for 20 minutes.

→ Make the mint oil by whizzing together olive oil and fresh mint in a food processor until you have a smooth, deliciously pungent liquid – this can be done at the time or as much as a couple of days in advance, but should be kept refrigerated.

→ After 20 minutes in the oven, remove the squid and heat the grill to its highest setting. Brush the squid all over with the mint oil and grill 4 inches or so from the heat source for 4 minutes before turning, basting with more mint oil, and grilling for a further 4 minutes. When ready, the flesh should have puffed out a little and turned opaque, while the filling will be hot throughout. Serve simply, with a drizzle of any remaining mint oil and fresh, light, steamed vegetables.

OYSTER SHOOTERS

> If you like your dinner quick and dirty, this is the dish for you. No commitment needed, just a quick jerk of the hand and it's over.

INGREDIENTS

2 oysters
2 tsp horseradish sauce
50 ml vodka

METHOD

→ Prepare the oysters as you would for Oysters on Ice. Remove each oyster from its shell and place in a shot glass. Add a tsp of horseradish sauce and top to the brim with vodka, which, ideally, should be ice-cold. Down the hatch with 'em, all in one go, and let the naughtiness commence...

OYSTERS ON ICE

If you're wild with hunger and can't hold yourself back, then don't be afraid to go au naturel: sometimes naked and raw is the best way. But if you're hovering on the precipice of 'too hungry', this easy recipe won't take long at all – a pinch and a squeeze and you'll be on your way.

INGREDIENTS

12 fresh oysters
24 ice cubes
2 lemons
Freshly ground black and
   white pepper
Tabasco sauce

METHOD

→ It is traditional to eat oysters raw, so only buy them from a reputable market and keep them chilled as constantly as possible, eating them on the day of purchase. Open them just before serving for the freshest taste of the sea: this isn't terribly difficult once you get the knack.

→ First, scrub the oysters well to remove any grit. Wrap a tea towel round your left hand and hold the oyster firmly in it with the flatter side uppermost and the hinge towards you. Carefully work the sharp edge of a broad, heavy knife into the crack between the shells as close to the hinge as you can find purchase. Twist the knife until the gap pops open (you'll need to use a little force), then work the knife around the shell. The halves should then separate easily. Discard the flat shells, leaving the oysters themselves in the saucer-shaped shell. Check for and remove any small pieces of grit or shell, then loosen the oyster away from the shell with a small, sharp knife.

→ Serve the oysters on a bed of crushed ice on a platter, interspersed with lemon segments.

→ How one should eat oysters properly is a matter for some debate, but you should provide Tabasco sauce and white and black pepper along with the lemon wedges. A squeeze of lemon, a dash of pepper and Tabasco, a forkful of oyster into the mouth, a sup of the juices from the shell with buttered brown bread to follow is most proper – but you'll probably find yourself knocking them back sans cutlery with a giggle and a grin.

GRILLED OYSTERS KILPATRICK

Peculiarly, this dish is also known as Angels on Horseback. Although angelic by name, bacon is sinfully delicious by nature; here it rides the oyster all the way to your tongue and melts in the mouth.

INGREDIENTS

12 fresh oysters
6 rashers bacon (streaky or
   back, but for best results
   use a similar amount of
   pancetta, thickly sliced)
12 tsp Worcestershire sauce
6 tsp unsalted butter
Black pepper, to season

METHOD

→ Preheat the oven to 200°C / 400°F. Prepare the oysters, separating the oyster from the shell as described in Oysters on Ice. For each half-shell, top the oyster with half a tsp of butter, a tsp of Worcestershire sauce, a smattering of black pepper and half a rasher of bacon. Place the shells on a baking tray and place them in the oven, near the top, for 8 minutes.

→ Meanwhile, heat the grill to a medium–high heat. Remove the oysters from the oven and place them under the grill for 2 minutes, just to crisp up the bacon a little. Serve the oysters in their shells.

STEAMY SAFFRON SNAILS

Snails: the other, other, other white meat. Not a dish to spring on your partner without discussing culinary boundaries first.

INGREDIENTS

2 tomatoes
1 red bell pepper
2 oz / 50 g celery, chopped
2 oz / 50 g unsalted butter
2 garlic cloves, peeled and
    crushed
A good pinch of saffron
    strands
2 tsp fresh thyme, chopped
2 tsp fresh sage, coarsely
    chopped
Salt, to season
24 shelled snails

METHOD

→ Skin the tomatoes (by immersing them in boiling water for a minute or so – then the skins should simply fall off with a little pressure) and deseed the red pepper. Chop both into chunks and put them in a food processor with the celery. Whizz them together for 5 seconds so you have a vegetable mixture that is coarse and chunky. Then, preheat the oven to 200°C / 400°F.

→ Next, melt the butter over a low heat in a heavy-based saucepan. Add the crushed garlic, saffron, thyme, sage and salt, and cook the mixture for about 2 minutes, or until the aroma of the herbs begins to waft gently from the pan. Mix the coarse tomato, pepper and celery mixture into the pan, stir well, and remove from the heat.

→ Arrange the snails in the bottom of an ovenproof dish (you can buy special ramekins in which to cook snails but a glass gratin dish will suffice), and cover them with the vegetable mixture. Place the dish, uncovered, in the middle of the preheated oven until the vegetables begin to brown slightly – this should take around 10 minutes, but certainly leave the dish in for no longer than 12, after which time the snails will begin to toughen. Serve immediately with Chablis or Chardonnay and sliced French bread.

CHEEKY CHICKEN AND MISCHIEVOUS MEAT

It can be all too easy to take chicken for granted. However, don't just give up on chicken all together – put the spice back into your relationship. Instead of careless encounters after work that are nothing more than a quick rub down with oil and 20 minutes of getting hot, do something really fresh and unusual.

Look outside the box when cooking up a meat dish, too; your interest can always be perked up by bringing something new into the kitchen. Red meat is vivid and primal in flavour; one bite and we're transported back through time to long, hot nights in our cave, when there was nothing to do but roast meat on the fire and whittle. But times have moved on and so should your tastes. Think plump, rotund balls, sitting glistening on a plate; a rich and vital mingling of pork and beef. Consider excitingly exotic Thai flavours and utterly traditional bangers, big platefuls and little nibbles. Oh! What a glorious thing meat is!

SPINACH AND RICOTTA STUFFED BREASTS

Picture a pair of plump, firm breasts quivering as you use your fingertips to push more and more white filling inside – that's what you could be having tonight.

INGREDIENTS

4 oz / 100 g washed spinach
2 chicken breasts
4 oz / 100 g ricotta cheese
¼ tsp nutmeg, grated
Black pepper, to season
2 oz / 50 g Gruyère cheese

METHOD

→ Preheat the oven to 200°C / 400°F. Bring a ¼ pan of water to the boil and steam the spinach over the boiling water for 2–3 minutes, or until it has wilted and reduced in volume a little. Remove it from the heat, drain well and gently squeeze out any excess water – a salad spinner is the best method.

→ As the spinach cools, take the two breasts, skinning them if need be, and make a slit in each one with the sharpest knife you have. Slice through the middle, along the length of the breast, forming a pouch. Take care not to cut all the way through.

→ Next, place the spinach in a bowl and add the ricotta. Mix the two together well and add a sprinkling of black pepper and the nutmeg. Spoon the mixture into the breast slits, stuffing it in well and pulling the upper tiers of chicken forwards to reclose the pouches. Place the stuffed breasts in a baking dish, adding a slight smear or spray of oil to the underside of each, and place them in the centre of the oven.

→ Remove them after 10 minutes, and grate the Gruyère over the top of the breasts. Return them to the oven for a further 10 minutes, check that the meat is thoroughly cooked, and then serve immediately with dressed rocket for ultimate pleasure.

STRAWBERRY-GLAZED
BREASTS

When they've been done correctly, these glazed breasts should be pale pink on the outside, as if flushed with exertion, and covered in a light sheen. The glaze is so tasty you may want to lick it from the breast, but refrain: the dish is best enjoyed as one.

INGREDIENTS

8 oz / 225 g strawberries
Juice and zest of 1 lemon
2 tbsp white wine vinegar
1 tbsp fresh mint, finely
    chopped (or 1 tsp prepared
    mint sauce)
Black pepper, to season
2 large spring onions, finely
    chopped
2 tbsp olive oil
2 large chicken breasts

METHOD

→ After putting aside a couple of strawberries to garnish the served chicken breasts later, purée the rest for about a minute in a food processor. If you want to get rid of the pips, mash them through a sieve with a fork. If you're feeling lazy, just do the food processor bit: the pips stay in, though I've never found a reason why this should be undesirable.

→ Mix the puréed strawberries in a bowl with the lemon juice and zest, vinegar, mint, a twist of pepper and the finely chopped onions, then whisk the olive oil in with a fork. Lay the chicken breasts in a baking tray and heap the mixture over the top. It's tastiest when prepared a few hours in advance, with the chicken refrigerated and marinating in the strawberry mixture before cooking.

→ To cook, preheat the oven to 200°C / 400°F and place the baking tray in the centre of the oven for 12–15 minutes, removing the chicken every 4 minutes to baste with the strawberry mixture. As with all chicken dishes, check the meat with a sharp knife to see if the juices from the centre run clear before serving (which may be difficult with this colourful dish – if in doubt, err on the side of caution).

→ As a final touch, crisp the glaze a little by placing the breasts under a hot grill for about a minute. Garnish with the reserved strawberries, a dash of the remaining marinade, serve with rice, smile, and look as sweet as you feel.

PORK, BEEF AND GARLIC ALBONDIGAS

2–4 | 10 | 20

This hot Hispanic dish will get your temperature rising. It puts an adult spin on the term 'finger food' with a plate stacked high with balls.

INGREDIENTS

4 oz / 100 g spicy sausages
4 oz / 100 g lean beef mince
2 shallots, finely chopped
2 tbsp fresh white breadcrumbs
2 tbsp fresh parsley, chopped (and a little extra to garnish)

1 large egg
2 large garlic cloves, peeled and crushed
Salt and black pepper, to season
Slug of olive oil
Tabasco sauce

METHOD

→ Slice the sausages along their lengths and remove the skins. Place the meat in a bowl and add the beef mince, shallots, breadcrumbs, parsley, egg, garlic cloves and plenty of seasoning. Mix the ingredients together well and with lightly floured hands shape the mixture into 13 even balls.

→ Heat the olive oil in a large frying pan over a medium heat. Add the meatballs (six at a time, depending on the size of your pan) and cook for 20 minutes, turning regularly and ensuring the balls are evenly browned. Slice a sample ball (hence you made 13 of them) through the centre to make sure it is cooked through before serving.

→ Remove the balls with a slotted spoon and place them on a warmed plate, sprinkling them with a little finely chopped parsley as a garnish. Serve with cocktail sticks and plenty of Tabasco, or a similarly spicy sauce, in a separate dish for dipping.

THAI TURKEY LOVE BALLS

2–3 | 40 | 20

These fragrant and flavoured balls are sure to spice up your evening. Make them to your pleasure; big balls that sit proudly atop the dish or smaller balls that you can fit in your mouth two at once. A word of advice: the bigger balls will need a little more heat and action before they're done.

INGREDIENTS

1 oz / 25 g caster sugar
2 tbsp fish sauce
1 red chilli, deseeded and finely chopped
1 stalk lemongrass, finely chopped
2-cm piece fresh ginger, peeled and grated or minced

12 oz / 300 g lean turkey mince
2 spring onions, finely chopped
1 tbsp cornflour
4 tbsp fresh coriander, finely chopped
Black pepper, to season
2 tbsp vegetable oil

METHOD

→ Heat together the sugar and fish sauce in a heavy-based pan over a low heat, stirring until all the sugar has dissolved. Remove from the heat and mix in the chilli, lemongrass and ginger. When cool, pour it into a mixing bowl with the turkey mince, spring onions, cornflour, coriander and a generous twist of black pepper. Mix well and then, with lightly floured hands, shape the mixture into even balls – you should get about ten from this quantity of meat. Cover the balls and refrigerate them for at least 20 minutes (this will help them retain their shape when cooked).

→ To cook the balls, heat the oil in a frying pan over a medium heat. Add the meatballs and cook for approximately 15 minutes, turning every 2 or 3 minutes. Cut a sample ball in half to check it is thoroughly cooked, i.e. no pink colour remains.

→ Dry the balls on a plate covered in kitchen paper. These balls are at their most amorous served with a gentle sprinkling of chopped spring onions, fresh coriander and a bowl of sweet chilli dipping sauce.

TOAD-IN-THE-HOLE

2 | 10 | 40

Can anything make you feel young again quicker than a big gleaming sausage nestled between two lips of mouth-watering batter? If you're feeling particularly greedy, see if you can fit two bangers in the hole at once.

INGREDIENTS

3 oz / 75 g plain flour
1 large egg
Salt and black pepper, to
    season
3 fl oz / 85 ml semi-skimmed
    milk
6 good-quality pork sausages
1 tbsp cooking oil

METHOD

→ To make the batter, sieve the flour into a large mixing bowl and break an egg into the centre of the flour. Add a generous pinch of salt, a fair old whack of pepper and a dash of milk. With a wooden spoon, blend these ingredients together, adding the rest of the milk little by little and stirring well, continuing the process with a whisk when the mixture is liquid enough. If there are any lumps, sieve the batter again to remove them. This mixture will also produce decent Yorkshire puddings (although if used for this purpose it should be allowed to stand for an hour – for Toad it doesn't really matter).

→ Next, preheat the oven to as hot as it will go (220°C / 425°F).

→ Lightly fry the sausages in a little oil until they are evenly browned, then place them in a baking dish with a tbsp of oil (or a little margarine), making sure the fat coats the dish evenly. Put the dish of sausages in the oven and when the fat is properly spitting-and-bubbling hot pour in the batter. Quickly return the dish to the oven and cook on the highest heat for 20 minutes, or until the batter has risen. When it has, turn the oven down to a medium heat and cook for a further 20 minutes. After this time the sausages should be thoroughly cooked and the surrounding batter fluffy but crisp.

→ Best served with a side portion of veg and some nice, thick gravy.

CARAMELISED APPLE PORK STEAKS WITH BRIE AND CIDER SAUCE

If you've been good this week, reward yourself with a good porking. These hunks of meat are covered with caramelised apple and promise sticky fingers, sticky mouths and that satisfied, almost-too-full feeling.

INGREDIENTS

2 large apples (cooking apples are best, but any will do)
2 oz / 50 g unsalted butter
2 oz / 50 g brown sugar
Slug of olive oil
4 pork escalopes, chops or loin steaks
4 oz / 100 g Brie cheese, cut into pieces

4 tbsp cider (dry or sweet)
2 tbsp crème fraîche
1 tbsp fresh sage, washed and finely chopped
Salt and black pepper, to season

METHOD

→ Peel and core the apples, then chop them into eighths. Melt the butter in a frying pan over a gentle heat and add the sugar, stirring the two together. As the sugar begins to dissolve and the butter bubble a little, add the apple segments and cook them, stirring occasionally, for 5 minutes, or until thoroughly golden and tender. Remove the apple from the pan with a slotted spoon and place it in a foil-covered bowl to keep warm.

→ Add the oil to the pan and heat over a moderate heat. Add the pork steaks and cook them for 5–6 minutes on each side, ensuring the oil is hot before you add the meat. Remove the steaks and place them on warmed plates. Quickly add the pieces of Brie to the pan and heat together with the cider.

→ When the Brie dissolves into the cider, remove the pan from the heat and stir in the chopped sage, crème fraîche and seasoning. Cover the steaks with the caramelised apples and top each with a spoonful of the cider and Brie sauce. Serve with a creamy mash to give your guest a proper seeing-to.

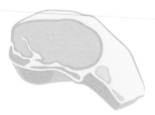

VOLUPTUOUS VEG, EROTIC EGGS AND SINFUL SIDES

Powerful stems thrusting upwards, standing proudly; roots pushing down into the dark secret crevices of the earth; cratefuls of thickness and girth being squeezed and prodded by the groping fingers of interested shoppers – vegetables are so invigorating. They can be a whole dish on their own or else they really complete a plate; who hasn't had a spring in their step after a night of meat and two veg?

If veg doesn't cure you of feeling tired and limp, try taking a big hit of protein. Eggs are one of the best sources of protein around; they're round and weighty and have so much goodness swimming around inside of them. They're versatile, too – you can take them as they come or whip them until they're light and fluffy.

The urge to have a bit on the side can seize any of us. Don't feel guilty – go for it. It will add spice and variety to your meal. There may be times when you wonder how you're going to squeeze everything in but you'll enjoy it too much to stop.

IMAM BAYILDI

2 | 15 | 50

This dish literally means 'the priest has fainted' and, indeed, who wouldn't when staring down at a bulbous purple aubergine; you'd be so keen to get it inside you that you would faint from anticipation. Don't worry: if an aubergine is too big for you to take in one go, this dish cuts it down and smothers it in dressing so you can take it bit by bit.

INGREDIENTS

6 oz / 150 g tomatoes
1 large aubergine
1/8 pt / 75 ml olive oil
1 white onion, peeled and finely chopped
2 large garlic cloves, peeled and crushed
1 green pepper, deseeded and chopped

Juice of ½ lemon (with the other half saved to garnish)
1 tsp brown sugar
1 tbsp fresh parsley, chopped (with a few sprigs to garnish)
1 tbsp pine kernels
Salt and black pepper, to season

METHOD

→ Prepare by heating the oven to 190°C / 375°F and skinning the tomatoes by immersing them in freshly boiled water for 1 minute, then pulling off the skins. Remove as many of the seeds as you can and chop the remaining flesh.

→ Slice the aubergine in half along its length and scoop out the flesh into a bowl. When doing this, leave a clear 2-cm margin of flesh behind, otherwise the skins will disintegrate when baked. This is where tradition states you're supposed to sprinkle the insides of the skins with salt and turn them upside down to drain away the 'bitter' juices, but I've never found this makes too much of a difference.

→ Heat half the oil in a saucepan over a moderate heat and add the onion and the garlic. Add the aubergine flesh, chopped tomatoes, green pepper, lemon juice, sugar, parsley, pine kernels, and a dash of salt and pepper. Reduce the heat and simmer the mixture for 15–20 minutes, until it begins to thicken. Remove the pan from the heat and spoon the filling into the aubergine shells. Place the shells side by side in a lightly greased baking dish. In a separate bowl, mix the remaining oil with an equal amount of water and a generous smattering of seasoning. Pour this mixture around (but not on) the aubergine halves, and bake them in the oven for 30 minutes.

→ This treat is splendid served both hot and cold, with a couple of lemon wedges for squeezing and a little parsley for looks.

NUT BALLS

You don't have to like meat to love balls; some people swear off the sins of the flesh but still love to pop a ball or two in the mouth and roll them around to get all the flavour. Whether you're meat-free or a meat freak, this mix is so tasty it will make your jaw ache.

INGREDIENTS

2 tbsp ground almonds
2 tbsp ground hazelnuts
2 tbsp ground pecan nuts
4 tbsp fresh white
  breadcrumbs
4 oz / 100 g Cheddar cheese,
  grated
1 large egg
4 tbsp sherry (dry is best) –
  and have the bottle handy
1 small onion, finely sliced

1 red pepper, deseeded and
  sliced into tiny chunks
6-cm piece fresh ginger,
  peeled and grated
1 tbsp fresh parsley, chopped
1 small red chilli, deseeded
  and finely chopped
Salt and black pepper, to
  season
1 lemon, quartered to serve

METHOD

→ In a big bowl, mix all the nuts, breadcrumbs and cheese together (with your hands is best). In a separate bowl, lightly beat together the egg and sherry, and mix in the onion, ginger, parsley, chilli and the pepper – which should be sliced up into tiny cubes or thin strips. Add this mixture to the nut and cheese mix, season the whole lot well and knead it all together.

→ The texture should be such that a half fist-sized ball should stay together in a cohesive lump. If the mixture is too dry and the ball simply falls apart, add sherry little by little. Remember: it's better to have too little moisture rather than too much, as the latter can be quite difficult to rectify afterwards. When the mix has a decent consistency, grease a baking tray and shape ten equal-sized balls from the mixture to place upon it.

→ Put the balls in the oven and turn it on (they need to heat up slowly rather than roast). Keep the heat low (180°C / 350°F) and cook for 25 minutes. Alternatively, they can be fried in a little oil over a low heat for a similar length of time.

→ Delicious served with a wedge of lemon, for squeezing, and a cooling sauce – perversely, tomato ketchup is excellent.

GARLIC AND BASIL BUTTER MEDLEY

The round head of a button mushroom grows plump and spongy as it soaks up all the butter. You really shouldn't play with your food, but they're so moist with smoky flavour that you'll want to run your tongue all over them.

INGREDIENTS

4 oz / 100 g unsalted butter
4-cm piece fresh ginger,
  peeled and grated
  or minced
4 garlic cloves, peeled
  and crushed

8 oz / 225 g button
  mushrooms, washed
8 oz / 225 g smoked tofu,
  cut into squares of ½-inch /
  1-cm sides
2 tbsp fresh basil, chopped

METHOD

→ Melt the butter in a heavy frying pan over a low heat. Add the ginger and crushed garlic to the pan, and fry very gently for 3 minutes. Add the mushrooms and cook for a further 5 minutes, until the mushrooms are soft. Add the tofu and turn up the heat just a touch, stirring carefully so as not to break the tofu cubes, for a further 2 minutes, then stir in the chopped basil.

→ Serve with a slotted spoon, but use a tbsp for extra buttery juice. A little squeeze of lemon juice, just at the end of the cooking time, provides an optional sharpening of the flavour.

NICELY SPICY SWEET POT AND BEAN PASTIES

2 | 20 | 35

You don't always need to go all in, all at once. The art of the tease is very welcome in the kitchen. Try these little pasties on for size – they tantalise and leave you wanting more. Perfect as part of a daring ensemble meal.

INGREDIENTS

1 large sweet potato, peeled and chopped into chunks
½ tsp chilli powder
½ tsp turmeric
½ tsp cumin
¼ tsp English mustard powder
Slug of olive oil
1 small white onion, peeled and finely chopped
1 garlic clove, peeled and crushed

2-cm piece fresh ginger, peeled and minced or grated
2 oz / 50 g French beans, chopped
1 tbsp fresh coriander, finely chopped
8 oz / 225 g shortcrust pastry
1 egg

METHOD

→ Bring a large pan of water to the boil and add the chunks of sweet potato. Simmer for 10 minutes until the flesh is tender. While it cooks, mix the chilli, turmeric, cumin and mustard powder together in a small bowl, and preheat the oven to 200°C / 400°F.

→ After 10 minutes, drain the sweet potato and allow it to cool. Heat the olive oil in a large saucepan over a medium heat, crush in the garlic, add the onion and fry them until soft. Next, add the ginger and the spice mixture. Continue to fry for a further minute, until the scent of the spices begins to waft vigorously from the pan. Add the sweet potato and beans, and 2 tbsp of cold water, and continue to cook for a further 5 minutes – by now you should have a nicely mashy mixture, with the green beans cooked and prominent. Stir in the coriander to the mixture, then remove the pan from the heat.

→ While the sweet potato mixture cools, divide the pastry into four pieces and roll each bit out into a circle on a lightly floured surface: it doesn't have to be an exact circle – near enough will do. Put one of the pastry circles on a lightly greased baking tray. Place a large spoonful of the cooled mixture on the centre of each pastry circle, adding more if there are any leftovers. Dampen the edges of each piece of pastry and bring the edges up to the top to make a Cornish-pasty-like shape. Repeat with the three remaining circles.

→ Finally, beat the egg and brush it over the pasties. Place them in the oven for 20 minutes, or until they are a crisp golden brown.

WHOLESOME ORANGE, YELLOW AND GINGER VEGETABLES

If you're feeling a little overwhelmed by all the changes in your kitchen, don't be afraid to go back to the comforting familiar; it doesn't have to be all-new, all the time, for a meal to be fresh and exciting. Sometimes all you need for a fulfilling evening is a big bed of parsnips and carrots to roll your meat around in.

INGREDIENTS

2 parsnips
4 carrots
2 oz / 50 g butter
4-cm piece of fresh ginger
½ tsp nutmeg, grated
Juice of 1 lemon

2 tsp caster sugar
1 tbsp fresh parsley, finely
  chopped, to garnish
Salt and black pepper,
  to season

METHOD

→ Wash and peel the carrots and parsnips, and slice them into thick pieces. Melt the butter in a large pan over a low heat and gently sauté the carrot and parsnip pieces for 4 minutes. Mince or grate the ginger into the pan, add a healthy grate of nutmeg, the lemon juice, and add enough water to just cover the veg.

→ Cover the pan with a well-fitting lid and allow the contents to simmer away for 20 minutes, by which time the carrots and parsnips should be tenderly soft and the liquid mostly evaporated. Increase the heat a little and spoon in the sugar, stirring and tossing the vegetables until they are coated with a glossy sheen. Serve sprinkled with a handful of finely chopped parsley and season to taste.

SWEET GLAZED SHALLOTS

Although they are small, the essence of a shallot is powerful and penetrating; it often brings a single tear to your eye. It will soon pass and you'll be crying tears of joy as you mop up the last of this tantalising dish.

INGREDIENTS

1 lb / 500 g shallots
3 oz / 75 g butter
2 tsp brown sugar
2 tsp English mustard powder
Dusting of paprika
Parsley, to garnish

METHOD

→ Allow the oven to heat to 180°C / 375°F. Peel the shallots, cut them in half and lay them, flat side down, in a baking dish. Melt the butter in a pan over a gentle heat and add the sugar and mustard powder, and finally ¼ pt / 100 ml of water, stirring until just below boiling. Pour this mixture over the shallots and dust the tops with a sprinkling of paprika.

→ Place the baking tray in the oven for 20 minutes, or until the shallots are richly glazed and glossy. Serve from a heated dish, garnished with a little parsley.

CREAMY CORIANDER CARROTS

Baby carrots may not be big but they sure are satiating; they just go to show that it isn't the size of your root but what you do with it that matters. The lightly ridged bodies of the carrots allow the lush liquid to pool on top and slide down the sides, immersing the vegetables in flavour.

INGREDIENTS

1 lb / 500 g baby carrots
2 tbsp single cream
2 tbsp fresh coriander,
    chopped
Black pepper, to season
Sprinkle of ground nutmeg

METHOD

→ Wash and trim the carrots and place them in a large saucepan with enough water to just cover them. Heat until the water begins to boil, then cover the pan, reduce the heat and simmer the carrots for 10 minutes. Then remove the lid, turn up the heat and vigorously boil the water until it has all been absorbed or has evaporated, shaking the pan to prevent the carrots from burning.

→ Remove the pan from the heat and stir in the coriander, cream and a generous twist of pepper. Transfer them to a warm serving dish, sprinkle over a little nutmeg (¼ tsp) and serve.

PUNCHY PORCINI RISOTTO

The strong nutty flavour of the porcini mushrooms in this dish will ravish your senses. Just when you think you're spent, get yourself a big, strong hunk of bread to mop up what's left.

INGREDIENTS

4 oz / 100 g dried porcini
   mushrooms
Good vegetable stock
   cubes or 1¾ pints / 1 litre
   vegetable stock
1 tbsp extra virgin olive oil
1 shallot, finely chopped

6 oz / 150 g Arborio rice
35 ml / half-bottle sherry (dry
   is best)
2 tbsp fresh thyme
2 oz / 50 g Parmesan cheese
Salt and black pepper,
   to season

METHOD

→ Add the dried mushrooms to a litre of vegetable stock in a saucepan. Bring it to the boil, then immediately reduce the heat so it simmers just below boiling point.

→ In a large, heavy-based saucepan, heat the olive oil over a medium heat. Add the shallot and sauté for 3 minutes, then add the rice and continue to cook for 3 minutes, stirring well to prevent the rice from sticking to the bottom. Pour in the sherry – leaving you enough left over for a couple of glasses – and continue to stir and cook until it has all been absorbed. Ladle in a couple of spoons of the hot stock, then reduce the heat under the rice slightly until the mixture is just simmering.

→ Remove the mushrooms from the stock with a slotted spoon. Coarsely chop them and add them to the rice, stirring them in well. Continue to add ladlefuls of the stock every few minutes until the rice seems to have absorbed all it can. The Italians say the perfect risotto cooking time is 22 minutes, and that the rice should be removed from the heat as soon as it is al dente – it's simpler to serve it up when it is good and creamy, with the thyme and Parmesan stirred in just at the end of the cooking period, and with salt and pepper added to taste. Not too many side dishes needed for this one as it's so rich and creamily wholesome – just a few hunks of crusty bread.

→ As porcini mushrooms are expensive, it's best to save the remaining infused stock for another occasion. Also, for those with electric hobs and those with an irrational fear of having to clean risotto rice from the bottom of the pan with paint-stripper who may be reading, if you keep the heat really low you should be all right. But if the worst happens and you find a layer of black crusted semolina at the base of your pan don't panic. Simply transfer the contents to a new saucepan and continue cooking.

MOUTH-WATERINGLY GOOD ASPARAGUS, RED PEPPER AND OLIVE QUICHE

Asparagus is delicious all the way from the base of the slender shaft to the tip, and it's no surprise that some people want to dispense with any formality and just swallow it down. If you can hold yourself back, envelope the asparagus in the silky folds of this quiche recipe for a filling all-in-one dish.

INGREDIENTS

2 oz / 50 g butter
1 medium white onion, finely
    chopped
3 large eggs
½ pint / 280 ml single cream
Sprinkle of nutmeg, grated
Salt and black pepper,
    to season

1 tbsp plain flour
2 oz / 50 g asparagus tips
2 oz / 50 g pitted green olives
1 red pepper, deseeded and
    finely sliced
1 x 10-inch / 26-cm part-
    baked pastry shell
2 oz / 50 g Cheddar cheese,
    grated
2 tbsp Parmesan cheese

METHOD

→ Preheat the oven to 190°C / 375°F and melt 1 oz (25 g) of the butter in a small pan over a low heat. Add the chopped onion to the butter and allow it to soften and discolour, stirring occasionally. When soft, remove the onion from the pan with a slotted spoon and put aside for later.

→ In a bowl, lightly whisk the eggs and cream together. Add ½ a tsp of salt, a good few twists of black pepper and a brisk grate of nutmeg – no more than ½ a tsp's worth. Scoop up a little of the mixture in a cup and add the flour, stirring until smooth, then pour this back into the bowl and mix well.

→ Arrange the asparagus tips, the whole olives and the deseeded and sliced red pepper in the pastry shell, ensuring an even spread of vegetables. Pour the cream, eggs and flour mixture over the top and sprinkle with the grated Parmesan and Cheddar. Cut the remaining butter into tiny chunks and sprinkle these over the cheese. Place the pastry shell directly on the middle oven shelf and bake for 25 minutes, then turn the heat down a notch and bake at 180°C / 350°F for a further 10–15 minutes, or until the surface of the quiche is a deliciously glossy golden brown. Great both hot as an invigorating midday meal, and cold as an al fresco appetiser.

PERFECT PESTO GENOVESE

If your meal is too dry and needs a little lubrication to help it slide smoothly down your throat, having a jar of pesto Genovese on hand will help you out of (or into) a tight spot.

INGREDIENTS

2 garlic cloves
1 oz / 25 g pine kernels
1 oz / 25 g Parmesan cheese
1 tbsp good white
   breadcrumbs
3 tbsp extra virgin olive oil
3 tbsp fresh basil (Genovese
   basil if you can get it)

METHOD

→ Peel and roughly chop the garlic cloves and throw them in a food processor with all the other ingredients. Whizz them all together in 10-second bursts until the mixture has a consistent yet coarse texture.

→ Serve with fresh pasta, or spread it on a pizza base as a delicious alternative to tomato sauce.

SIMPLE TRUFFLE EGGS

From walnut to fist, truffles come in all different sizes – it's really up to you to decide how much you can handle, and the price you're willing to pay. Their flavour is so strong and overpowering, even the smallest amount will infuse the dish. In this recipe, the truffle combines with the egg to send your taste buds into ecstasy.

INGREDIENTS

4 medium eggs
*2 oz / 50 g dark or white
  truffles*
1 tbsp crème fraîche
*Salt and black pepper,
  to season*

METHOD

→ To keep the eggs and truffles moist, the best way to cook this dish is to heat the eggs over hot water, in the same way you might melt chocolate. So, bring a large water-filled saucepan to the boil. In a second saucepan or bowl (which needs to be slightly smaller so it can sit in the boiling water), gently whisk together the eggs and season lightly. Slice the truffles and add them to the mixture.

→ Place the smaller saucepan over the boiling water and stir the mixture until it begins to thicken – this may seem like it takes forever, but in reality it only takes 5–6 minutes; just make sure you keep stirring the whole time.

→ Remove the thickening mixture from the heat and stir in the crème fraîche. Serve immediately, spread thickly on toast.

VODKA CAVIAR FETTUCCINE

Why not take experimentation in the kitchen one step further and introduce role play? You are a Russian oligarch, used to having the best, and your favourite refreshments are vodka and caviar. Where does your evening go next? You decide…

INGREDIENTS

1/3 pt / 250 ml single cream
1 garlic clove, peeled
Zest of ½ a lemon
1 oz / 25 g unsalted butter
2 tbsp Parmesan cheese, grated
2 tbsp vodka (or, alternatively, Marsala)

Slug of olive oil
Salt and black pepper, to season
8 oz / 225 g fresh fettuccine
2 oz / 50 g salmon roe
1 tbsp fresh chives, finely chopped

METHOD

→ Heat the cream in a heavy-based saucepan over a moderate heat, adding the garlic clove – leaving it whole but squished with the back of a heavy knife – and lemon zest, and bringing the pan to the boil. Reduce the heat slightly but continue to allow the cream to boil until it has thickened and reduced by about a third of its original volume.

→ Remove the garlic clove and lemon zest with a slotted spoon and add the butter to the cream, cut into chunks, and the grated Parmesan cheese, and whisk the mixture lightly until smooth. Allow the contents of the pan to simmer for 2 minutes before removing it from the heat and stirring in the vodka and a big twist of pepper.

→ Meanwhile, bring a large saucepan of water to the boil, adding a good pinch of salt and a drizzle of olive oil. Add the fettuccine (or your favourite pasta – this will work just as well with something like linguine) and boil until al dente after 4 minutes – or as per packet instructions if cooking dried pasta.

→ Drain the pasta, place it in a large bowl and stir in the salmon roe and the cream sauce. Serve immediately whilst piping hot, with a handful of chopped chives topping each plate.

POTATO AND EGG BREASTS

Big, round golden potatoes topped with peaks of egg yolk, these munchable mounds are warm and inviting. This recipe calls for firm, smooth mash, but if you like it a little lumpy that's your personal preference.

INGREDIENTS

1 lb / 500 g floury potatoes,
   e.g. King Edward
1–2 tbsp semi-skimmed milk
1 oz / 25 g unsalted butter
Salt and black pepper, to
   season
2 large eggs
2 oz / 50 g Cheddar or
   Gruyère cheese, grated

METHOD

→ Preheat the oven to 200°C / 400°F. Bring a large pan of water to the boil and add the washed potatoes, cut into quarters. You can peel them first or cook them in their skins, which will fall off after they're cooked – whichever you find most convenient.

→ After 20 minutes the potatoes should be tender and mashable. Drain them well and leave them in the pan with a tea towel covering them for 2 minutes. Then add the butter, milk and a twist of seasoning (a little salt and plenty of pepper). The mash consistency you're aiming for is smooth but firm – i.e., a spoonful of it, lifted from the bowl, should stay on the spoon. The best way to achieve this is to add the butter and milk little by little so you don't go overboard.

→ Grease a baking tray and divide the mash into two mounds upon it. Press down the centre of each mound with your fingers, to form a well. Carefully (yolk intact now...) break an egg into each well and top each egg with a sprinkling of grated cheese. Place the baking tray in the oven for 20 minutes – or until the eggs are thoroughly set and the potato is beginning to turn a slightly crispy gold. Serve hot with a wry and cheeky smile.

VEGETARIAN GREEN CURRY (WITH JASMINE RICE, OF COURSE)

If you like to finish your evenings hot, with skin tingling and sweat dripping down your neck, then you're in for a treat with this Thai curry. Silken tofu, supple vegetables and creamy coconut milk all work in tandem to bring this dish to a head.

INGREDIENTS

8 oz / 225 g smoked tofu, cut into small cubes
2 tbsp dark soy sauce
4 oz / 100 g bamboo shoots
1 green pepper, deseeded and cut into strips
Slug of vegetable oil
1 tbsp green curry paste

½ pint / 280 ml coconut milk (you can also use creamed coconut with hot water)
1 tbsp peas (frozen is fine)
4 oz / 100 g beansprouts
1 tbsp fresh coriander, roughly chopped
1 spring onion, finely sliced, to garnish

METHOD

→ While you chop up the pepper and bamboo shoots, allow the tofu cubes to marinate in the soy sauce for 20 minutes or so. Heat the oil in a wok or saucepan over a medium heat and add the green curry paste, frying it for 1 minute. Add half the coconut milk and the drained tofu, green pepper and bamboo shoots.

→ Continue to cook these at the same temperature for 5 minutes, stirring gently and occasionally, taking care not to break the tofu cubes. Add the remaining coconut milk, the peas and the beansprouts. When the curry comes to the boil, reduce the heat and allow it to simmer away for 10 minutes.

→ Just before serving, stir in the chopped coriander, and serve in bowls garnished with a little sprinkle of chopped spring onion. This isn't a curry unless it's served with steaming hot traditional Thai jasmine rice that you can buy from any good supermarket.

BUTTERY MASH WITH PARSLEY AND NUTMEG

Even if your arm aches as you drive the head of your masher into the yielding folds of the potato over and over again, summon that last reserve of stamina and push through; you will be well rewarded.

INGREDIENTS

10 oz / 250 g floury potatoes,
  e.g. King Edward
2 oz / 50 g unsalted butter
1–2 tbsp semi-skimmed milk
1 tbsp single cream
1 tbsp fresh parsley,
  finely chopped
Salt and black pepper,
  to season
½ tsp nutmeg, grated

METHOD

→ Simply peel, halve and boil the potatoes for 15–20 minutes or until they're soft and mashable. Drain them well, and leave them for a minute in the pan with a tea towel over them to absorb the steam.

→ Mix in the butter, milk, cream, parsley and a good twist of salt and pepper, and mash it all together until it has a smooth, creamy consistency. Add the nutmeg, stir it in well and keep it all warm until ready to serve.

SUMPTUOUS SAVOURY VEGETABLE PURSES

2–4 | 15 | 35

The buttery folds of the pastry clench tight around the cheesy stuffing, imprisoning the hot vegetables and ensuring no juices escape. The purses look tantalising enough on your plate, but the surge of heat and aroma as you penetrate them with your knife will tip you over the edge.

INGREDIENTS

8 oz / 225 g courgettes, thinly sliced
4 oz / 100 g French beans, cut in half
8 oz / 250 g broccoli, sliced
2 oz / 50 g margarine
Good slug of olive oil
10 12- x 6-inch sheets of filo pastry

6 oz / 150 g feta cheese, cut into cubes
Salt and black pepper, to season
1 tbsp fresh thyme, chopped
1 tbsp fresh tarragon, chopped
1 egg, beaten

METHOD

→ Preheat the oven to 190°C / 375°F. Prepare the vegetables by steaming them for 5–7 minutes – this will work well in a stackable steamer as you can do them all at once. Leave them to cool and melt the margarine in a pan over a very low heat. Add a good slug of olive oil and brush the mixture lightly over five of the filo sheets – then stack these on top of one another.

→ Shaking free any excess moisture, put the steamed vegetables in a bowl and mix in the cubed feta cheese. Season with a little salt, a big twist of pepper, and add the thyme and tarragon. Divide this mixture in half and spread one half of it over the surface of the stacked pastry, making sure there is a clear 2-inch margin of pastry spare around the edges. Roll the pastry into a tube from the long side (like a Swiss roll) and fold in the short edges. Brush the surface with the beaten egg and place the 'purse' seam side down on a well-greased baking tray.

→ Repeat the process with the other half of the veg mixture to make a second purse, and bake them both together for 30–35 minutes, or until the outside of the pastry is a crisp golden brown. Leave the purses to cool for a couple of minutes before serving, sliced and garnished with a flower.

DECADENT
DESSERTS

Even if you think you're filled to the brim, there's always room for one more, as the cook said to the parson. If you've had a heavy session, something fruity, light and teasing may be the treat to get your gander up again. Or perhaps it's one of those nights of pure indulgence; you want to get fuller and stickier and messier and finish on an orgy of chocolate and cream. Here are some recipes to suit every fancy; you could even have a couple on the table at the same time…

CHOCOLATE LICKING AND DIPPING SAUCE

Bitter, thick and lingering, you can dip anything you like into this sauce (provided it's cooled enough first) or else tip it out and let it ooze over the treat of your choice. With a pleasant burn as you swallow, the addition of rum will stoke the fire inside of you.

INGREDIENTS

8 oz / 225 g dark, bitter or
  cooking chocolate (the best
  quality)
2 tbsp golden syrup
2 tbsp espresso coffee
½ pint / 300 ml single cream
1 tbsp dark rum

METHOD

→ Break the chocolate into pieces and put them in a heavy-based saucepan with the golden syrup, cream and coffee. Heat the pan very gently, ideally suspended over another pan a quarter full of gently simmering water. Stir continuously until all the chocolate has melted, the consistency is even and the texture glossy. Stir in the rum and remove the pan from the heat.

→ Use immediately, nice and warm, or store refrigerated in an airtight container for up to a week, mixing well and heating gently before use.

SPOTTED DICK

4 | 20 | 120

Though perhaps unlovely at first glance, as you discover the satisfaction a spotted dick can bring you'll start to find the thick doughy pudding, engorged with raisins, pleasing to the eye – and mouth.

INGREDIENTS

4 oz / 100 g lightly salted
   butter (or unsalted and a
   pinch of salt)
8 oz / 225 g self-raising flour
4 oz / 100 g raisins
2 oz / 50 g caster sugar

METHOD

→ Fold a large square of baking parchment or greaseproof paper so it is double thickness and lay it on a baking tray. Take a little chunk of the butter and melt it in a pan over a low heat. Brush or smear it all over the parchment.

→ Sieve the flour into a bowl, cut the butter into small chunks and mix it into the flour with your hands. Mix in the sugar and raisins, then knead in 4 or 5 tbsp of water until you have a soft dough. Remember it's best to add too little water to start with, rather than putting in too much initially.

→ On a lightly floured surface, roll out the dough into a short, thick cylinder. Place the dick on the greaseproof paper and wrap it securely but loosely, sealing the ends with string or rubber bands. Place the dick package in a steamer with a well-fitting lid and steam for 2 hours.

→ Serve with lashings of custard, naturally.

SIMPLE MANGO SORBET

Mangoes are tantalising if you're lucky enough to pluck them straight from the tree, but they're just as lusty if the grocer is your source. The animalistic urge is to part the skin and press your mouth to it, half consuming the flesh and half drinking the juices. However, if you have guests, perhaps this sorbet is the preferred route to take.

INGREDIENTS

2 lb / 1 kg ripe mango
2 tbsp demerara sugar
2 tbsp gin
12 ice cubes
Pinch of salt

METHOD

→ Peel the mangoes, remove the stones and pulp the flesh in a blender together with the sugar and 1½ pints / 750 ml water. Add the gin, ice cubes and a pinch of salt and whizz it all together until the consistency is rough but even. Pour it into a frozen metal container (or, failing that, a plastic food storage container) and freeze for 1 hour.

→ Unlike ice cream, the formation of ice crystals is a must for sorbet, so there's no need to keep taking it out to stir, but give the sorbet a good mash before serving.

CHAMPAGNE ICE CREAM

This creamy dessert is so heady and delicious you could simply open your mouth, tilt back your head and let it slide over your tongue and down your throat. Its fizzy finish will go straight to your head.

INGREDIENTS

½ pint / 300 ml single cream
2 oz / 50 g caster sugar
2 egg yolks
Zest of 1 lemon
½ pint / 300 ml whipped
   cream
2 flutes' worth of champagne

METHOD

→ Heat together the single cream, sugar, egg yolks and lemon zest in a heavy saucepan over a low heat, and stir continuously until the mixture comes to the boil. Remove the zest with a slotted spoon and remove the pan from the heat. When the mixture has cooled, fold in the whipped cream and the champagne.

→ Transfer to an ice-cream maker, turn it on and let it go about its business. If you do not have such a device, place the mixture in a pre-frozen metal container (or plastic food storage container). Put the container in the freezer for an hour, removing it every 15 minutes to stir well with a whisk – this is to stop ice crystals forming, which will ruin the texture.

→ Serve with wafers, the last of the champagne, and eat lovingly from spoons, fingers, thighs and navels.

COFFEE ICE CREAM

The pulse of caffeine in this cool coffee dessert is guaranteed to make your pupils dilate and your blood race; however, it is the intense flavour that will leave you short of breath.

INGREDIENTS

4 egg yolks
4 oz / 100 g caster sugar
Pinch of salt
1 pint / 600 ml single cream
2 tsp vanilla essence
1 small cup espresso coffee
2 tbsp coffee-flavoured liqueur

METHOD

→ Lightly whisk together the egg yolks, sugar and a pinch of salt. In a separate saucepan, mix the cream, vanilla essence, coffee and liqueur. Gradually add this coffee-cream mixture to the egg yolks, stirring continuously. Heat this mixture in a bowl or saucepan over another saucepan of simmering water, stirring continuously until the mixture begins to thicken a little – when ready it should be thick enough to coat the back of a spoon.

→ Allow the mixture to cool and transfer it to the chilled bowl of an ice-cream maker – let it do its stuff until the ice cream has set. Alternatively, if you don't own such a machine, freeze the mixture in a plastic food storage container for 1 hour, removing it every 15 minutes to give it a good whisk.

→ For an extra cool touch, serve scooped into bowls, garnished with a sprinkling of coffee beans and a sprig of mint.

HONEY AND LEMON BAKED FIGS

For proper instructions in the art of eating a fig, try following D. H. Lawrence's poem:

> 'The proper way to eat a fig, in society,
> Is to split it in four, holding it by the stump,
> And open it, so that it is a glittering, rosy, moist,
> honied, heavy-petalled four-petalled flower.'

INGREDIENTS

6 figs
4 tbsp clear runny honey
Juice and zest of 1 lemon

METHOD

→ Heat the oven to 200°C / 400°F. In a bowl, cover the figs with the honey, add the lemon juice and zest, and mix the whole lot up so the figs are well-coated.

→ Pour the figs out into a baking dish, separating the fruits from one another, and drizzle any residual honey and lemon mix over them. Place the baking dish in the oven and cook for 20 minutes. Serve steaming hot with a scoop of vanilla ice cream or some crème fraîche.

DECADENT CHOCOLATE MOUSSE

This dessert is so rich and decadent that you only need a little amount to bring your meal to a climax. It is important to savour it; dip the tip of your spoon very lightly into the surface of the mousse and drag slowly across the chocolate, then raise to your lips to suck the sweetness into your mouth.

INGREDIENTS

4 eggs
2 tbsp caster sugar
8 oz / 225 g chocolate (your choice of milk, cooking or dark – but always buy the best quality stuff available)
2 tbsp liquid black instant coffee
4 oz / 100 g unsalted butter
2 tbsp brandy

METHOD

→ Separate the egg whites and yolks and save both. Whisk together the yolks and 1 tbsp of caster sugar in a bowl until thoroughly combined.

→ Break the chocolate into small pieces and melt it in a bowl or saucepan over another saucepan containing gently simmering water. Add the coffee and stir continuously until you have a smooth chocolate liquid. Chop the butter into pieces and gradually add it to the chocolate, beating the mixture with a whisk. When all the butter has melted and the mixture is smooth and even, add the egg-yolk mixture, continuing to whisk constantly and patiently until the mixture thickens after 5 minutes or so. Remove the bowl from the heat, fold in the brandy with a spoon, and allow the mixture to cool.

→ While the chocolate cools, whisk the egg whites and the other tbsp of sugar together until it forms soft, fluffy peaks. You could do this by hand if you have wrists of steel and incredible patience but a better option is to use an electric whisk or beater. When the chocolate has cooled, fold in the egg whites with a spoon. Do this gently, but thoroughly, trying to maintain the aerated structure of the egg white mix as much as possible.

→ When thoroughly combined, spoon the mixture into individual serving dishes. It won't seem like you have much per person but it is incredibly rich so a little should suffice. Place the dishes in the fridge to set for at least 2 hours, or overnight. Serve topped with a little grated chocolate, or a sprinkling of crushed Maltesers or Flake bars.

GUAVA JELLY (FOR RUBBING 'PON YOUR BELLY)

A meal doesn't have to be intense and serious to be delightful, especially when there is such fun to be had in bouncing and jiggling around with this jelly.

INGREDIENTS

3 lb / 1.5 kg guava
Juice of 3 lemons
Juice of 1 lime
Granulated sugar
2 tbsp dark rum

METHOD

→ Wash the fruit and inspect the outside for any bruised or damaged bits, which you should then cut out and discard. Slice the whole fruits (no need to peel or core them) into thick chunks and place them in the largest saucepan you can find. Add the lemon and lime juices and enough cold water to cover the guava flesh entirely. Heat the liquid to boiling point, then turn down the heat a notch so the liquid simmers away. Leave it like this for 30 minutes, or until the liquid has reduced by about a third – the guava flesh should by now be soft and squishy.

→ Remove the pan from the heat and strain the guava flesh through a sieve, a jam bag or a clean nylon stocking, collecting the juice underneath. Really squidge up the guava so you get as much juice out as possible. The flesh can now be discarded. Measure the collected liquid in a measuring jug and return it to the pan. For every litre (2 pints) of liquid add 1 kg (2 lb) of sugar. Bring the liquid back up to boiling point, stirring it up to dissolve all the sugar. Add the rum and boil vigorously for a further 2–3 minutes, skimming any foam from the surface, until it develops a thick consistency – this stuff should set by itself, as guava contains plenty of pectin. Pour the liquid out into jelly moulds or glasses (which should be sparklingly clean or sterilised), cover with cling film and refrigerate for 1 hour. Liven yourself up and serve – spoons not strictly necessary.

CHOCOLATE STRAWBERRY EXPLOSIONS

What are pink, perky and fit perfectly in your mouth? Strawberries, of course! But these strawberries contain a secret surprise – when you bite into them they squirt delicious liquid down your throat. It can be fiddly, pumping the berries full of liqueur by hand, but well worth it.

INGREDIENTS

8 oz / 225 g fresh strawberries
8 oz / 225 g dark, bitter or
  cooking chocolate (the best
  quality chocolate available)
75 ml orange-flavoured
  liqueur

METHOD

→ Preparing the strawberries is a delicate operation, but an easy one if you kit yourself out well beforehand. You'll need as many toothpicks as you have strawberries, some polystyrene in a block, oh, and a syringe. If you don't have the latter you'll have to leave out the 'surprise' element, but if you don't have polystyrene to hand it's easy to improvise.

→ Wash the strawberries but leave them whole (with stalks intact), and spear each one with a cocktail stick through the stalk end. Melt the chocolate by breaking it into chunks in a saucepan or bowl, and placing it over another pan of gently simmering water. Mix the chocolate as it melts until it is completely smooth. Remove the chocolate from the heat and dip each strawberry into it, swirling each one as you do so, so that about half of every strawberry is covered with chocolate.

→ Leaving the strawberries resting on anything will spoil the effect, so to ensure the chocolate shells harden intact, spear the cocktail sticks into a suitably yielding surface. What's that? You have a block of polystyrene right there? Perfect. Otherwise, an old tissue box turned upside down, Blu-Tack or even a bar of soap should do the trick. Place the array of strawberries in the bottom of the refrigerator for at least 20 minutes (this will harden the shells).

→ Before serving, use a syringe to inject the centre of each strawberry with a squirt of liqueur, arrange them alluringly on a dish and feel waves of warmth and satisfaction envelop you as your dinner guest marvels at your culinary kudos.

CREAMY PANNA COTTA WITH RASPBERRY BUDS

When testing if the dessert is set, give your bowls a little shimmy; a good panna cotta will have a little wobble to it. The sweet mounds should have a silken sheen, especially when wet with amaretto.

INGREDIENTS

2 pints / 1.2 litres double
    cream
2 vanilla pods
3 gelatin leaves
6 fl oz / 150 ml full fat milk
6 oz / 150 g icing sugar
120 ml / 4 fl oz amaretto (or
    liqueur of choice)
6 oz / 150 g punnet of
    raspberries, washed

METHOD

→ In a heavy-based saucepan, heat 900 ml / 1½ pints of the cream and the vanilla pods together until boiling. Simmer until the liquid has reduced by a third of its volume. Remove the pods (carefully – they'll be hot!), open them out with a sharp knife and scrape their insides into the cream.

→ Meanwhile, soak the gelatin leaves in the cold milk for 15 minutes. Remove the gelatin and heat the milk until boiling. Replace the gelatin and stir well until it has all dissolved. Pour the milk through a sieve into the cream, stir well and leave the mixture to cool.

→ Whisk the icing sugar into the remaining cream and fold it into the cooled cream mixture. Mix in the amaretto, setting a little of it aside for later. Go on then, and a glass for yourself. Pour the mixture into two moulds of roughly 200 ml volume (bowls will do), and refrigerate for at least 2 hours to allow the mixture to set. Turn out the bowls onto dessert plates, garnish with raspberries, a drizzle of amaretto, and serve.

HONEY PIE

Lemon, orange, sweet honey – don't you want to just have a taste of that pie? The woozy, hot inside of this dessert is full of nuts and sweetness, just like a pie should be.

INGREDIENTS

8 oz / 250 g honey (clear is best)
6 oz / 175 g chopped pecans (or walnuts or almonds)
Zest of 1 lemon
Zest of ½ orange
6 tbsp dark rum
10 oz / 300 g shortcrust pastry (if using frozen make sure it's thawed)
2 tbsp caster sugar
1 tbsp semi-skimmed milk
Yolk of 1 egg

METHOD

→ Preheat the oven to 200°C / 400°F. Gently heat the honey in a saucepan. When hot add the pecans (you can use walnuts, almonds or just about any nut, but pecans are the best) and orange and lemon zests and stir to coat the nuts well. Add the rum, stir well and remove the pan from the heat.

→ Halve the pastry and roll it out until it is thin enough to line a 20-cm pie dish, or any similar sized ovenproof dish. Sprinkle the sugar over the pastry lining and spoon the sticky honey mixture on top. Roll the remaining pastry out to form the lid, seal the edges and decorate the top with any offcuts you may have.

→ Finally, brush the lid with a gently whisked mixture of egg yolk and milk, pierce the lid with a knife in five or six places, and bake in the oven for 30–35 minutes, or until the pastry is golden brown.

→ As the honey filling retains its heat well, it's best to let the pie cool for 10 minutes before serving. Vanilla ice cream is simply and absolutely a must.

AMOROUS
ALCOHOL

There's no better way to end the day than with a nice big fat cock... tail. Or a slim, long cocktail. Or with a shallow, round cocktail. Some of them are pink and fruity, some of them are dark and spicy. Some need a lot of preparation, others you just have to give a quick shake and you're on your way. There are times you want to take three or four in a night and times that just one leaves you sleepy and satisfied. To summarise, any day that ends with a cocktail is a good day. Here are a few delicious cocktail recipes to give your day a happy ending.

BLACK VELVET

As usually happens when something earthy and strong meets something refined and flirty, there's a lot of passion in this cocktail. Opposites attract and make magic on your tongue.

INGREDIENTS

Irish stout (such as Guinness or Murphy's)
Champagne, chilled

METHOD

→ Fill champagne flutes half full of stout. Top up with chilled champagne.

SEA, SUN AND... SANGRIA

MAKES 4

If you haven't had a chance to roll around in the sand, hot, sticky and covered in a light sheen of sweat, then allow this delicious summer tipple to recreate the feeling for you.

INGREDIENTS

1 bottle Rioja or similar red wine
50 ml Havana Club rum, or Bacardi
Juice of 1 lime
2 oranges
1 lemon
Ice

METHOD

→ Cut the lemon and oranges into chunks and put them in a jug that will hold a litre of liquid. Add the lime juice and rum, and top up with wine. Serve over ice in glasses, with a wooden spoon in the jug so you can strain out the fruit.

BETWEEN THE SHEETS

A naughty, sharp and wonderfully strong cocktail classic that leaves little to the imagination.

INGREDIENTS

Juice of 1 lemon
50 ml brandy
50 ml triple sec
50 ml light or Havana Club rum

METHOD

→ Pour all the ingredients into a cocktail shaker over plenty of ice. Shake well, strain into two cocktail glasses and serve garnished with a twist of lemon peel if you want to be really classy.

PORTUGUESE HARD-ON

MAKES 2

We all need a stiff drink on occasion and a Portuguese Hard-On certainly fills that criteria. Cool to the touch but burns inside you – this is quite the treat.

INGREDIENTS

50 ml vodka
50 ml peach schnapps
Lemonade

METHOD

→ Fill tall glasses with ice, add equal measures of vodka and peach schnapps, and top up with lemonade – as simple as that.

LONG, SLOW, COMFORTABLE SCREW (UP AGAINST A COLD, HARD WALL)

MAKES 2

A quickie cocktail is good but there's an old-school charm about the long, slow, comfortable screw.

INGREDIENTS

25 ml vodka
25 ml sloe gin
25 ml Southern Comfort
25 ml Galliano
25 ml amaretto
Orange juice

METHOD

→ Combine the alcoholic ingredients in a cocktail shaker and pour them over cold hard walls of ice in long glasses. Top up with orange juice and serve.

SCREAMING ORGASM

MAKES 2

I'm not sure this one needs too much introduction. Guaranteed to produce an orgasm of the tastebuds, a Screaming Orgasm is delightfully smooth and seductive.

INGREDIENTS

25 ml vodka
25 ml amaretto
25 ml Bailey's Irish Cream
25 ml Kahlua

METHOD

→ Simply mix together all the ingredients and serve in whiskey tumblers over cracked or crushed ice.

PASSIONFRUIT BELLINI

Two aphrodisiacs – champagne and passionfruit – in one glass, plus a little Dutch courage? Just see where the night goes.

INGREDIENTS

4 ripe passionfruits
50 ml Cointreau
1 bottle champagne

METHOD

→ Halve the passionfruits and scoop the flesh into a sieve. Gently force the flesh through the sieve with a fork or spoon, collecting the resulting purée in a jug. Add a generous 50 ml of Cointreau to the purée and mix well. Dollop a tbsp of the mixture into each glass – use champagne flutes for authenticity – top up with chilled champagne and serve.

VANILLA BRANDY

They say the older the fiddle, the sweeter the tune and that's certainly true if you leave this concoction to build flavour over time.

INGREDIENTS

70 cl bottle good brandy
2 vanilla pods

METHOD

→ Score the vanilla pods down the centre and put them straight into the brandy bottle, sealing it tightly. The brandy's flavour will improve with age, but will still be deliciously potent after about a week if you keep the bottle in a cool, dark place.

VANILLA SMOOTHIE

A creamy smoothie crammed full of ripe 'n' ready bananas and sticky, runny honey.

INGREDIENTS

4 ripe bananas
½ pint / 300 ml natural yogurt
½ pint / 300 ml semi-skimmed milk
1 vanilla pod
2 tbsp runny honey
8 ice cubes

METHOD

→ Peel and chop the bananas and put them in a food processor with the yogurt, milk, honey and ice cubes. Cut the vanilla pod open and scrape all the seeds and sticky bits in, then whizz all the ingredients together until the consistency is even and the texture smooth. Serve immediately in long glasses.

GLÜHWEIN

MAKES 4

Get close by the fire with this toe-tingling, blush-bringing, spicy concoction.

INGREDIENTS

1 bottle red wine
Zest of 1 lemon
Zest of 1 orange
4 whole cinnamon sticks

4 whole cloves
2 tsp freshly ground nutmeg
1 tbsp honey

METHOD

→ Find a square piece of muslin – or even a stocking, sterilised in boiling water – and tie it up with the cloves, cinnamon, lemon and orange zest and nutmeg inside. Pour the bottle of wine into a large saucepan, add the muslin spice pouch, and heat the wine over a low-ish heat, turning it down if it looks as if it'll start boiling. Add the honey and let it dissolve. Infuse the wine for 5 minutes, taking care not to let it boil, and serve warm. There should be enough spice in the pouch for another bottle, if the fancy takes you.

THE A–Z OF
RUDE FOOD

I hope the recipes in this book were enough to give you that gentle push you were begging for, and that you're now sliding, hopelessly enraptured, down that slippery tunnel into a world filled with erotic recipes, wonderfully arousing aphrodisiacs and decadent, romantic meals. If, to complete your newfound skills as Mr or Miss Lover Lover (mmm), you're looking for a list of smarmy conversational ploys or smooth chat-up lines and seduction techniques, then I really can't help you, having never been too good at those myself. I can, however, hand over to you all I've discovered about rude food throughout my painstaking research. All that eating, all those frolics… it was hard work, I can tell you. Please take this dictionary of filthy aphrodisiacs and rude food trivia and venture forth, with my blessing, into a new era of naughty food-filled sexperimentation…

ARTICHOKE

These are as sensual to prepare as they are to eat. You can buy artichoke hearts in jars and tins, ready for use. Artichokes are extremely tasty if not incredible to behold. If you can get hold of fresh artichokes you'll have a world of fun peeling back the outer leaves, dipping your fingers into the delicate cup and softly stroking the glowing heart within as it peers out from its prickly protection.

ASPARAGUS

Eating one's first asparagus spear is something of an epiphany: the moment the bulbous head disappears between your lips, oozing globules of melted butter… it's enough to make anyone come over all unnecessary. Rich in vitamins and minerals, asparagus is certainly a healthy treat, as well as making for an erotic eating experience. Be warned, though: asparagus is guaranteed to make you smell. Did we get that at the back? Or was I being too coy? Your bodily fluids, semen and vaginal lubricant, in particular, will smell of sweet, green vegetable matter – though this is not, as you might first think, entirely unpleasant.

AUBERGINE

A thoroughly indecent vegetable. Thick, phallic and arrogant, the aubergine makes a bold statement, yet inside, its flesh is crisp and pristine. When cooked, it turns into a creamy morass that screams sex from the rooftops.

AVOCADO

Perhaps the sexiest foodstuff of all time. They possess curves that are voluptuous yet not obscene, and to eat a perfect, ripe, buttery one is in itself an experience matched only by orgasmic bliss. Well, perhaps that is pushing it a bit, but they do have a history of getting people ready for action as it were.

The Aztecs named the avocado *ahuacatl*, which roughly translates as 'lovely bollock', and in their culture it was such a symbol of fertility and rampant bonking that a village's brides-to-be were kept safely chaste and locked away during lovely bollock gathering season – which is quite understandable.

These days everyone is free to feel the curve of its dinosaur hide, the satisfying schlurp of the stone slipping out and, above all, the smooth sensuality it adds to a host of dishes. Best of all, though, is avocado at its simplest – halved, stoned and served with a drizzle of vinaigrette.

BANANA

They're sweet, creamy, gently curved and between 6 and 10 inches long. Do I have to spell it out? Perhaps because of this they have been used for centuries as a symbol of temptation and debauchery. Bananas are also an incredibly good source of vitamin B and slow-release energy – perfect for tennis matches and sexual triathlons – and are at their most incredible best if slit open, stuffed full of chocolate, wrapped in foil and oven-baked or barbecued.

BASIL

Long regarded as a herb with special medicinal properties in Eastern civilisations and revered throughout the Mediterranean, basil is an essential ingredient in a whole range of dishes. I can't claim that my research has revealed it to have any particular aphrodisiac effects, but it is damn tasty – in the subtle, hinting way that means you notice, desperately, its absence rather than its inclusion. The sweeter, oriental varieties are great for Thai cooking, and kept in a pot as a growing herb it adds a warm, clean aroma to rooms – enough to make you think you're in Marrakesh.

BAY LEAF

With a gentle wafting dream of a flavour, one or two bay leaves added to a sauce and removed before serving can turn something bland and unexciting into a hintingly cheeky romantic dish.

BRAZIL NUT

Brazil nuts are the chunkiest nuts there are. Aside from the gentle sway in their hips, they are thought to be a good source of selenium, which helps stimulate endorphin production and leaves us feeling healthy all round.

CARDAMOM

The seedpods have a deliciously warm and spicy flavour that works incredibly well with milk to leave you feeling happy and soothed, making cardamom a perfect pre-bed or breakfast ingredient. Indeed, Hindu recipe books have treasured this spice for centuries, suggesting that the ground pods, boiled in milk with a little honey, make a knockout impotence cure for men. There may be something in this, as randy scientists have identified cineole contained within the sexy little pods, and this stuff is known to stimulate the central nervous system.

CARROT

Although carrots contain a touch of myristic acid – the purportedly hallucinogenic and mood-altering component of nutmeg – they are no longer thought to possess any specific aphrodisiac qualities. In the past, carrots were feasted upon by Middle Eastern royalty, believing they provided stamina for those long Arabian nights spent pleasuring the harem, and, of course, good night vision is always an advantage.

CELERY

It is chiefly the seeds of the humble and unassuming celery plant that have a history of use as an aphrodisiac. The Romans in particular were fond of celery, dedicating the plant to Pluto, who was their favourite god of sex. We now know that celery is packed full of vitamins A, B and C and stimulates the pituitary gland, which has the important responsibility in our body of releasing sex hormones.

CHILLI

Chillies come in a wide and sometimes bewildering array of shapes, sizes and strengths. What they have in common is a dose of capsaicin, reputed to provide a euphoric, natural high, and a supply of vitamin C. Chilli – especially dried, such as the fearsome and erroneously named cayenne pepper (*capsicum annuum*) – also acts as a releaser of endorphins, from which their reputation as an aphrodisiac probably derives. Be warned though: put too many of these babies in a dish and you'll spend the evening crying, and making camp and cartoonish faces at one another as you go steadily redder.

Milk and alcoholic drinks will take away some of the sting from over-chillied tongues and lips – water will do absolutely nothing, unless you are Wile E. Coyote, in which case it will make steam issue forth from your ears.

CHOCOLATE

If you've not worked out that sex and chocolate are interlinked then you've been missing all the fun – as well as all the not-so-subtle hints the advertisers have been dropping since you were little. Anyway, there seems to be some scientific basis to chocolate's reputation as a wicked aphrodisiac. Firstly, it is packed with caffeine which, as coffee and cola drinkers will know, helps to shuffle you forward from the back of the sleepy shelf right to the precipice of mental alertness. But that's not all: chocolate is also rich in phenylethylamine. That's easy for you to say, you think. Phenywotsit – which we'll call PEA – is best described as a natural amphetamine and antidepressant, and is produced within our own bodies when we are in love. Hence chocolate can be warming, soothing and, yes, sexually arousing.

Now, some of the reputation chocolate has may, scientifically speaking, be a load of old cobblers reiterated ad infinitum by the advertising community, but its position as a comfort food, in rituals of courtship, and especially as a sauce to be licked and nibbled from everywhere imaginable, makes chocolate a rude food like no other.

CLOVE

The Chinese, who purportedly first used cloves in cooking, and the Romans both believed in the curative and aphrodisiac powers of cloves. Today, cloves are used principally in desserts, where they make us feel warm, happy and slightly fruity.

COCO DE MER

I've never tasted one so I have no recipes for the giant nut of the palm *Lodoicea maldivica*, but it deserves a mention as it holds the coveted honour of being the world's largest fruit, and it is also quite simply the world's rudest. This massive nut, which can weigh in at anywhere up to 20 kg, resembles a woman's lower torso in exquisite anatomical detail. Furthermore, the nut's jelly-like flesh is famed locally for its powerful aphrodisiac properties. Ladies and gentlemen, we have a contender for the rudest food ever.

Unfortunately, coco de mer nuts are not generally available in your local supermarket, unless you live in the Seychelles.

COFFEE

Brewed from the roasted beans of *Rubiaceae coffea*, the drink we know as coffee can be both a soothing comfort and a jolting and invigorating kick-start. It is thought to increase blood flow, heart rate and mental alertness – all of which also occur when we are sexually aroused. A nice coffee after a meal is delightful, but it does not necessarily need to be caffeinated as the ritual is often enough. Indeed, my heartfelt advice is to drink coffee in moderation, not just because a reliance upon it will ultimately cause you stress and you will become unhealthy, but because after two double espressos even the owner of the steadiest hands imaginable will become a jittery bag of fidgets.

CORIANDER

This herb has been used throughout history as an aphrodisiac, but my own experiments were scuppered by my abundant overuse of it. There are only a few dishes that aren't enlivened by a handful of fresh, chopped coriander, and it is especially sexy in hot and spicy Indian and Thai dishes, giving them a cool yet tangy air of sophistication.

CREAM

An incredibly sexy food to cook with because it has a smooth and slinky version of the Midas touch, turning all it touches to velvet. However, it truly comes into its own when it is taken out of the kitchen and into the bedroom, maybe with some strawberries, maybe as ice cream, and licked from every smooth and wrinkled surface you can find. Especially fun and manageable whipped – an evening spent with your partner and a can of the UHT stuff could be one of the best evenings of your life…

EGG

It is difficult to find a more obvious symbol of sex. While eggs provide a source of protein and help contribute to a healthy, balanced diet, there is not really any compelling evidence that they are, in themselves, aphrodisiacs. However, including them in a romantic meal may add to the poignancy of the moment – proving to you both that life is a cycle, that sex is natural, sex is good, that not everybody does it, but everybody should. Now I feel a song coming on – look what you've made me do.

ESCARGOT

Snails. Perhaps, while they are alive, it can be argued that these are not the sexiest of creatures – indeed, many people harbour a fear of the undulating, slimy, home-carrying snail quite out of proportion to any real threat it poses, and being captured by a speedy, house-sized, carnivorous and hungry snail is a common childhood nightmare. Or was that just me?

Nonetheless, snails are famous as an aphrodisiac delicacy, and are often served with garlic butter so powerful that most concerns about taste and texture are simply blown away.

FENNEL

A massive body of scientific research suggests that – along with pumpkin – the aroma of liquorice is one of the most effective food turn-ons for both men and women. Certainly a claim worth investigating, and even if untrue you'll have lost nothing, as the slightly ovoid and peculiarly hand-shaped fennel bulb makes a delicious addition to creamy soups, while the seed works well with fish.

FIG

While the fig is a strangely unforgettable fruit, it hardly seems to exude instantly sexy charisma. However, closer examination reveals the skin to have a throbbing hue, as if something fearsomely rampant has been locked away inside and is looking for day release. Gently slice one open and you'll see what all the fuss is about – a beautifully moist, red-pink flesh radiates out from a central orifice exuding the sweetest aroma ever. Figs were Cleopatra's favourite fruit: say no more.

GARLIC

Garlic gets a lot of bad press. Despite its evil- and vampire-warding qualities, there is often a tendency to hang negative connotations on garlic's distinct and pungent aroma. This has not always been so: cultures around the world and throughout history, from the Ancient Egyptians to the Japanese, have employed garlic as an aphrodisiac, as well as using it for its curative properties.

There is little doubt today that garlic is a kitchen essential, and a rude food cook without some would be no kind of rude food cook at all, for it provides a certain special kick and oomph to the simplest of dishes. My personal trials – which I can hardly claim to have conducted with scientific rigour – have demonstrated that garlic enlivens the senses and makes you feel that little bit more alive. And, yeah, it smells: just make sure your partner has some, too.

GINGER

This curiously gnarled root has been used for centuries as an aphrodisiac throughout the Indian subcontinent and Asia, and is widely recommended by herbalists today as a cure for impotence. Despite its appeal as an essential ingredient in Chinese and South-East Asian cooking, it is worth noting that its sexual association is not peculiar to the Orient. The practice of baking gingerbread men originated in Europe as part of a ritual aimed at landing eligible maidens a suitable husband.

HAZEL AND HAZELNUT

Hazel has strong associations with pre-Christian pagan rituals. At May Day time, the festival historically known as Beltane, the women of the villages had their private parts twanged, stroked and thwacked with hazel rods in the hope that some of the fertility god Donar's prolific sexual prowess would, er, rub off on them. Meanwhile, hazelnuts were used as a representation of the phallus in rituals. It is not surprising that ancient aphrodisiac recipes for potions and so forth relied heavily on the roasted nuts or the oil derived from them. Hazel is still a symbol of fertility, as the hazel bush is one of the first to come into flower in the spring, and science tells us that hazelnuts are rich in vitamin E, which is associated with normal sexual function. They are also a tasty nibble.

HONEY

Where would we be without this stuff? Try to imagine if you'd never tasted it – no, if it had never existed at all. Honey symbolises lightness, sweetness and sticky, messy love, and has done since humankind first discovered it. It features in the *Kama Sutra*, has been recommended as an aid to sexual health by everyone from the Ancient Greeks through to modern-day Hindus and, of course, tradition states that newlyweds should seclude themselves after their wedding day to free them temporarily from the shackles of society, drink honey potions and make long, lingering love until the next new moon – a tradition we still practise today when we take honeymoons. So if you're in for a sexy weekend (or fortnight, if you're lucky), at least make sure you take a jar of the runny stuff along.

ICE

If you've never taken your lover to bed armed with little more than a box of ice cubes, then I suggest you stop reading this book right now and get to it. But I won't tell you what to do with them – that would spoil the fun.

MANGO

While mangoes have an incredibly vibrant colour and a unique, fibrous flesh, the sexiest thing about them is actually eating them. A truly ripe mango eaten in the correct manner (with the skin slit lengthways from top to tip, quartering the fruit, the flaps peeled away one by one, and the flesh juicily devoured) provides a slurping, sticky spectacle with many opportunities for lingering looks and naughty finger sucking.

MUSTARD

Use this wickedly spicy crop for the purpose nature surely intended – a dollop of the good English stuff for wonderful sausages, grainy French for perfect beef, and smooth Dijon for just about anything, but especially creamy mash and velvety salad dressings.

NUTMEG

Nutmeg is an extremely versatile ingredient. It can be used to spice up just about anything, and its warm, round and yet lingeringly tangy flavour is unique, powerful and heartening. It also contains myristic acid, a chemical which could be the reason for its reputation as a potent aphrodisiac.

If you love nutmeg – and it is an easy nut to fall for – my advice is to invest in one of those little graters with a small container at the top for holding the nut. The other advice I would offer is to remember that not everyone will share your passion: use nutmeg only sparingly (no more than a pinch or two in any dish), as it can easily overwhelm all other flavours.

ONION

As the Roman author Martial said in AD something or other, 'If your wife is old and your member exhausted, eat onions aplenty'; although he was never too clear as to whether this would give the said organ fresh wood, as it were, or merely put off the old other half's amorous advances. Onions are, however, mentioned extensively in Ancient Arabic and Hindu love manuals; it is traditional for French newlyweds to be served onion soup on the morning after their wedding (to revive those flagging libidos, presumably); and there is evidence that Ancient Egypt's high priests were banned from going anywhere near these pungent, multi-layered balls… so make of that what you will.

OYSTER

The three things people most commonly associate with oysters is that 1) they taste horrible, 2) they are fearsomely potent aphrodisiacs and 3) that Casanova ate bucketloads of them each morning in the bath. All three of these statements could be true in their own ways. Oysters certainly have a unique taste, and not everyone will like them. They taste, essentially, of the sea in a fresh, briny sort of way, and swallowing them whole will not change this fact or make it easy to ignore. So, if they're not your bag, they're not your bag.

Their power as an aphrodisiac, meanwhile, will really depend on who you're with when you eat them, remembering that love is possibly the best aphrodisiac – although it may run a close second behind sheer unbridled lust. Oysters are low in fat, high in protein and are an excellent source of zinc, which helps produce testosterone and of which a supply in the body is vital for normal sexual functioning. International opinion is largely agreed that they do the trick. As for the highly-sexed Casanova – well, he can't have done that every morning, can he?

PARSLEY

Gone are the days when that little sprig of parsley was left on the side of the plate, wondered at by all inexperienced diners. Should I eat it? And, if not, why is it there in the first place? For a rude food meal – especially one that looks like it might lead somewhere else – the parsley should really be eaten, as it has the effect of sweetening up your secretions be you a man or a woman. This could be especially helpful if you've just eaten a load of asparagus or garlic, foods with a reputation for making your bodily juices smell.

PEPPER

Black, ground and crushed; green and whole; white, light and fragrant – pepper is to rude food cookery what gold is to Fort Knox. Invest in a good grinder – it will be worth it.

I don't think there's any need to go as far as the Ancient Arabic penis expansion recipe, which suggests grinding it up with lavender, honey and ginger, and rubbing the stuff all over the, ahem, longitudinally challenged member-in-question.

PINE NUT

The kernels from pine cones were waxed lyrical by the poet Ovid and were prescribed by Ancient Greek doctors to treat impotence. They have been putting the warm, nutty kick in pesto for centuries.

QUINCE

Forget passionfruit and pomegranates – quince is the fruit with the sexiest history. Dedicated to Aphrodite by the Ancient Greeks, and to Venus by the Romans, quince is one of the oldest known fruits, having been grown throughout the Mediterranean since 300 BC at least, and there is some evidence to suggest that the apple mentioned in the Bible is none other than the saucy quince pear.

Quince is traditionally eaten at weddings, perhaps because the seeds and the mucilage (or sticky) cells of the pear are thought to make it a potent aphrodisiac.

RICE

An Eastern symbol of fertility, and one of the world's oldest cultivated crops, rice is far from a mere staple. It is thrown at weddings to bless the couple with a happy and fruitful relationship, and in Japan and China, eating rice from the same bowl as your beau is used to signify engagement, while rice wine (sake) is a key component in Japanese marriage ceremonies.

ROSE

Roses are symbolic of all we know to be good and uncomplicated in romance, yet at the same time they are intricately complex, delicate flowers. Fortunately, they're not just for show. The soft, inner petals can be washed and sprinkled into salads to add a gentle yet lingering fragrance.

SAFFRON

Weight for weight, saffron is one of the most expensive substances in the world. It is made from the stigma hairs of a small crocus – as each crocus has three stigma hairs, and 1 oz of saffron requires something in the region of 15,000 hand-picked hairs, the cost is hardly surprising. Its reputation as an aphrodisiac is, however, without parallel: it is quoted as a vital sex aid in Arabic, Hindu, Roman and Greek love manuals, and its warm red glow gives some dishes the little boost they need.

SPINACH

This, of course, is the stuff that Popeye made famous. Spinach is, as we all know, a good source of vitamins and iron, but that's no reason to go eating the tinned stuff, which is invariably disgusting. Fresh spinach makes for light and fun eating, is superb in salads and, when steamed and reduced a little, can be stuffed into all sorts of unlikely places.

Beware, though, of the classic First Date Pitfall: stay well clear of the stuff or bring a good sturdy toothpick because if it can get stuck between your teeth, it will.

STRAWBERRY

Strawberries are the most sensual of the summer fruits. Sweet and juicy, strawberries are not only delicious but also good for you, being packed with vitamin C and having very few calories. Of course, they are also erotically nipple-like, especially when they're covered in sugar and cream and pushed between your lover's lips. To add flavour to the cream, add a drop of vanilla essence and a sprinkling of icing sugar before whipping it.

Strawberry season is early summer, so pack a hamper with the one you love and pick your own. If you come across the tiny, wild variety (*Fragaria vesca*), have a good, long nibble on those, too.

SWEET POTATO

Sweet potatoes are incredibly tasty. Underneath the face they present to the world – that rough, gnarled and grotty skin – is a lurid flesh that is a delight to reveal, boil and mash. As a comfort food I think they beat their tuber relative, the potato, and are much prettier. Sweet potatoes, and their cousins (yams) turn out to be brimming with a chemical called diosgenin, which mimics the effect of female sex hormones, and hence is used in all sorts of aphrodisiac potions.

TOMATO

You say 'tomayto', and may well have 'tomarto' hurled back in response, but the Italians prefer to consummate their long-running affair with the tomato by giving it a sexy name: *pomodoro*, or love apple. However, it should be remembered that the Italians, with their staple of pasta and sauce, were not always the tomato's friend: the Romans tried to ban the tomato because they thought it was poisonous. Enjoying a slightly better press these days, the tomato is certainly a sexy fruit (although it tends to masquerade as a vegetable in supermarkets), and since it is red – the colour of passion and the colour of love – it is an essential addition to your forays into rude cookery.

It is a statistical truth that 79 per cent of the population have had a tin of economy peeled plum tomatoes in the back of one of their cupboards for over a year. Isn't it about time you got yours out?

TRUFFLE

The truffle seems an unlikely choice as a symbol of wealth, power, indulgence and decadence, as it is small, crinkled and dark. It is certainly not a sexy object in itself, and although there is a certain teasing androgyny about the apparent lack of a food category in which to place it, it is in fact a sort of tuber. This places it roughly in the potato family, and on top of this slight, truffles are usually located by using trained pigs that were, only minutes before, snuffling around eating each other's poo.

Against these culinary black marks is the incredibly dense, rich and nutty flavour the truffles provide when grated into any dish (but especially eggs and omelettes, cream and pasta sauces). Truffles are the kind of thing you might buy on holiday, thinking it a good idea at the time. It's worth knowing what to do with them, because they do taste delicious. Alternatively, you can buy bottles of truffle oil, usually olive oil infused with the taste of the little blighters – this stuff makes a delicious accompaniment to shellfish dishes.

VANILLA

I read somewhere that vanilla pods are such a good aphrodisiac that they were named after the female sex organs (with the Spanish word for vagina being markedly similar). I'm not sure as to what extent this is bunkum, but there could be something in it. Vanilla is remarkably pleasant to smell and inhaling its delicious aroma has a mood-changing effect, rather than vanilla being an aphrodisiac food, per se.

WALNUT

Poor Jupiter must have received quite a ribbing from his fellow gods, for these gnarled, wrinkled nuts are named after his testicles – hence the Latin name (*Juglans regia*) that slyly refers to Jupiter's Balls. The Roman tradition of throwing these at wedding ceremonies (where rice would usually be thrown) still persists to this day, while saucy minx Cleopatra ate sphinx-sized portions of them, believing they would increase her libido. As if she needed any help!

THE WORLD'S CRAZIEST
DRINKING
GAMES

QUENTIN PARKER

THE WORLD'S CRAZIEST DRINKING GAMES

Quentin Parker

ISBN: 978 1 84953 947 0

£9.99

Are you bored of Beer Pong? Is your Ring of Fire more like a ring of embers? If so, this book is exactly what you need to shake up your next party.

Ever since its discovery hundreds of years ago, alcohol has valiantly taken on the role of 'ice breaker', bringing people together through silliness and shared hangovers. While it's true that the feel-good factor of alcohol is a global phenomenon, not everyone in the world plays Fuzzy Duck or Centurion at their parties.

This collection of the truly bizarre and outrageous games played by drunk people around the globe will add sparkle to any night out (or in). Your new favourite drinking game is waiting for you within these pages.

If you're interested in finding out more about our books, find us on Facebook at Summersdale Publishers and follow us on Twitter at @Summersdale.

www.summersdale.com